THE HABITS REVOLUTION

Learn in 10 Steps how the Power of Tiny Changes
Can Transform Everything in Your Life

DAMON FOGG

TABLE OF CONTENTS

INTRODUCTION

There is a tendency to shape, change and reduce habits. For people, what is machine automation? They reduce the time it takes to respond to an event and reduce the energy needed to think about the reaction. They bring significant benefits if used well. Otherwise, they charge a toll. We must not only learn to change habits but also take into account the practices that have developed or evolved. Patterns are neurological and biochemical. After all, habits are under the control of the conscious mind, but not directly. This book describes the anatomy of an obsession and sheds the necessary light on how patterns work to transform the highest gross potential into success and success. Everything you are about how you like coffee, anxiety and the size of your biceps or stomach is a function of your compelling profile. A single action or decision currently causes none of us. Our position and respect, which we have travelled so far, are based on habits that we develop throughout our lives. If you are happy with your situation and want tomorrow to be the same as today, you don't have to change anything, and your habits, no matter what, take you there. There are many more possibilities in you than what you just discovered or set on fire. There is much more to you than what you showed the world. The only way to unlock and unlock this potential is to throw an arc that will take you to your destination. You cannot do this with conscious thought. Applying conscious thinking to each step will stop you and limit your potential. Have you ever seen a tennis champion get up, watch the next volley and think about options, ask yourself what to do and plan? No. Use the habit of years of practice to get close to the ball without even thinking about it. Patterns are a function of three essential elements: trigger, action and reward. A necessary habit arises when all three parts are fulfilled. This happens as soon as the first instance of the trigger, the work and the repetition occurs. As the sequence repeats for each action, the habitat attacks more until it occurs deeply rooted in the fact that the conscious mind no longer needs to pay attention to it when running in the background. All this happens due to the evolution of the brain over time. During this time, the brain discovered that the most effective way to use the power of the brain is to divide the psyche into conscious and unconscious processes. Both are particularly necessary. The conscious mind is designed to act in the present and support the five senses.

The subconscious has been designed to deal with the rest. The power of the second is much higher than the power of the first. For the same reason that the mind cannot contemplate the incoming tennis ball, it does not understand its speed, trajectory and rotation, nor can it predict how to hook the ball with a racket so that the ball is returned in the most favorable way for the player. "Opponent. Entry, calculation and execution take place in a fraction of a second. Only the subconscious can handle this speed. The conscious cannot. For this reason, he fights when he is forced to perform these tasks. Millions of algorithms of individual habits work in the subconscious mind from the moment he wakes up in the morning and retires at night. Everyone has a target and focuses on his trigger. When someone detects his trigger, he performs a sequence that responds to that trigger. Therefore, this sequence controls the actions themselves, because now it becomes a priority. When you drive a car and pedestrians suddenly bounced in front of you, involuntarily apply the brakes because it is an algorithm triggered by the trigger. By the time you're not listening to the radio, you don't think about the brakes, you don't think about the coffee in your lap, just stop by emergency, habits make a conscious effort without permission. When a trigger occurs, the pattern simply takes control. All these things, which are taken for granted, coffee in the morning, tying shoelaces or walking, can be done without the slightest contribution of the conscious mind.

But be careful, it turns out that the subconscious does not distinguish between habits. The psyche collects all the patterns that meet these three essential elements: trigger action - reward. The trigger is an opportunity. It is possible to win a prize. The bonus will come if a person commits an act. Because the subconscious mind does not distinguish good from evil when it returns to habit, it does not allow it to disappear, although it can be harmful. It is power in its most basic form: a rare and dispassionate distinction between good and evil.

The purpose of this book is to use this power and direct it to things that can raise our lives to the level of the stratosphere, in whatever field we want. It is not always about fame, power and money. Of course, we can use the control of habits to generate wealth, gain energy and achieve stardom. But the strength of addiction can do more.

HOW DO HABITS WORK?

Habit sequences are part of almost all mental processes. A habit is simply a conserved reaction to a stimulus or series of incentives. Parallel to the programming would be the equivalence of the computer with "If-then-then-do-it" with an additional event that can be considered a reward for strengthening this sequence. Think of habits as a three-step process. Indicate the signal followed by the action that ends with the prize. Award Signal Action CAR Several texts describe more detailed passages and have longer progress, but only observe these three elements to obtain a functional understanding of the process. The signal is like a trigger. This event or object initiates a cascade of other activities that cause the action. An easy way to see how it works is to imagine an insect bite. When it itches, it is a sign. This signal causes a response. When you scratch the Sting bug, it's action. When you scratch, the feeling you feel is a reward. The CAR sequence ends with a feeling of happiness that attracts the senses and awaits another feeling of joy. The next time the itch appears, the body will react faster. When this system goes crazy, some look for an opportunity to snack and then scratch after happiness. It doesn't matter where the signal comes from or who administers the prize. If the sequence is completed, the brain will try to repeat it. The mind creates an algorithm that looks for a trigger to avoid wasting time in action as soon as the signal is activated. Rewards can be activated internally or externally. After internal activation, the leading mind manages the awards. In particular, one of the neurotransmitters controlled by the primary brain, dopamine, is activated by the lid of the abdomen (VTA) and floods the frontal lobe as a reward.

For external activation, the process is slightly different. The external reward that accumulates causes a chemical reward released by the primary brain in the frontal cortex. The central brain tries to enslave the cerebral cortex, offering pleasure as a reward. This reduces willpower to combat the needs of the original mind. Diets help illustrate the underlying dynamics. The problem is to follow a diet. Not because the body needs food, but because it is difficult to break the habit of eating. The central brain that controls the rest of the body makes me feel that the dieter is desperate to eat.

But in most cases, the person is more than capable of depleting food for the day, and even 2. The discomfort results from the primitive brain, which forces addiction. Can provide positive amplification or negatives. The diet and dietary dimensions of nutrition and energy intake are an effective way to observe your habits. On the one hand, it is a practice used to support life. But, as we have seen, it can go too far. When a habit appears in the primitive brain, it forces the frontal cortex to reduce its opposition to everything it wants. Over time, the addiction creeps into other areas of life. We do not live in isolation. Everything we experience exists on a three-dimensional plane and is connected. When a person finds habits, he can join other areas of life without his knowledge or consent.

Get into the habit of Pavlov's dog. The experiment was conducted by a physiologist, Nobel laureate, Ivan Pavlov. He began trying to show that dogs secrete saliva when they see food. To prove this, he and his team of researchers put a glass of glass in the dog's mouth to collect secretions. It worked. The dog's saliva was secreted when the food appeared. However, the most exciting thing is that the dog began to secrete saliva every time a person serving food appeared. To go further, Pavlov decided to call every time the food was served. What he found became the basis for research in many areas of physiology. After a few moments of ringing the bell while serving food, the dog drools when the bell rings, even when no food is served. In the experiment, the signal was transmitted from the menu to the sound. The dog accumulated many years of relationship between fed food and the beginning of the digestive process. The sequence of association and its position can also be observed in other areas of the human psyche. This habit drag can be used to change the habit or change it completely, as we will see in the following chapters.

The structure of the brain and ease of use The human brain is built so close to the dimensions of the chain link. Every neuron in the brain is connected to many other neurons. Because of this, when a person is not focused, one memory can free another memory and confuse the problem. Emotions and mentality can be the same. If you detect a familiar perfume in the air, it is good to remember the person you associate with that perfume. When memories are encoded in mind, they do not arise in isolation. Consciousness is associated with something the mind already knows. Therefore, it is compared with a metal fence. If you have played a combination of words, you will see that mentioning one name activates the memory of another name. The more connections a memory fragment has, the easier it will be to recover it because there are many paths to achieve. Pawłów's dog shows that memory, the smallest particle of a habit, is created by combining all directly responsible elements something is also related to that on the periphery. When the dog remembered the time the food was served, he coded it as the person who served it and pressed the bell. When one of these events occurs, it also causes a reaction. If you have a particularly persistent habit, you can be sure that your memory has also associated this trigger, action or reward with something other than the core of the practice. If you can discover what it is, you can begin the process of changing your addiction to one method and transferring it to another through these paths of association. We can have total control over our practices if we decide. For this reason, the art of reflection turns out to be a worthy companion, even when our lives are going well, especially when our lives are in disarray. The power of meditation resides in each of us, and sometimes it can also become a self-critical conversation in the head. This is counterproductive. However, the ability to reflect consciously and systematically is something that controls the formation of habits without conscious effort or stress. The mind has several filters derived from values and beliefs. These systems of values and beliefs will reject practices that infiltrate other areas, if possible. If someone adopts a bad habit, there is a good chance that he knows that it is terrible, but he has not joined the two sides of the case: the one who knows what is wrong and the page that models the habit. When someone thinks, a regular pattern that appears will become a habit, and that is enough to reverse the training. Let's start talking about how habits arise: the three-step CAR process. This is an easy way to maintain the training process. Then we saw how it could be monitored, and the reason for this phenomenon is the structure of the brain. It is also essential to understand the mental trait called neuroplasticity.

WHAT YOU WILL LEARN DURING THE
REVOLUTION OF SMALL HABITS

The revolution of little practices consists of seven parts of rapid movement. Each of them is an integral part of the discussion. Each of them will prove to be crucial for developing good habits that will remain. That said, I organized the material so you can easily access the selected section at any time. You will notice that the summary is full of details. Navigating this activity guide will be very easy if you decide to jump from one section to another.

BRAIN PERCEPTION

It's time to stop wasting effort and energy on habits that don't appear anywhere, or worse, delay it. Get rid of these habits and replace them with habits that will take you there, in which you dare not just your dreams. Change these old habits, replace them with new ones in just thirty days and see how it works. To do this, you need to understand your mind and its motivation. You should worry more about the mind between brain and mind. There is a brain; then there is a mind. They are not the same. The brain is the physical matter that you see when you look inside the skull. It is grey, white and has a creamy texture. On the other hand, the mind is not something that can be seen if you look inside. The mind is built on the brain. The brain is tangible: it can lift it, it has weight, volume and consistency. The mind is irrelevant. You cannot hold it, touch it or see it, but you can feel its effects. Your mind consists of all experiences, conditions, habits and perceptions. Your brain is full of all neurons, dendrites and axons that carry electrical signals. Your mind is full of thoughts that arise in the brain by the flow of these electrical signals. All these electrical signals animate our thoughts and memories. When electrical activity stops, there will be no more thoughts or memories. These electrical impulses are transmitted at an extremely high speed, almost at the speed of light, so sometimes we can evoke thoughts so fast that they almost seem to come out of nowhere. To live in a physical world characterized by the movement of physical objects, we must reduce part of our mind at this speed. The part of the mind that has been designed to work more slowly and adapt to the speed of the physical world is called the conscious mind. The subconscious moves too fast for the conscious mind. When we say "I" or "we," it generally means that we mean the conscious mind because these are the "we feel" thoughts. You don't feel the habit. Just do it. So, instead of telling (the conscious mind) to do this or that, it makes more sense to install it as a habit and let the stronger side of the brain take care of it and do it. The brain began as a group of nerve endings at the dawn of evolution. Electrical wires from all parts of the body moved around the spine and converged at the base of the skull, where they joined the vertebrae. Millions of years ago, this grouping from the base with nerve endings could only have a life support function? Coordinated physiological tasks to allow adjustment and development of life. On an evolutionary scale, as new species evolved and different functions emerged, the brain grew more and more. For your convenience, you should see the brain in this evolutionary layer as part of a group of nerve endings, and then build the primary brain and then the cerebral cortex ("neo" means new). You can think of three areas of the brain, from the oldest located deep in the base to the youngest, which borders the skull wall. Brain development shows exactly how we become what we are now. The deepest part of the brain governs our biological func-tion. The upper layer, the main brain, managed survival and expan-sion. And finally, the outermost layer allows cognitive thinking and imagination. There is a unique relationship between all due to the way they are layered. The upper brain (the one in the outermost part of the periphery) is the place where we try to reach our higher self. This is a new bark. The medium gives us our basic instincts: food, sex, aggression, fear, etc. This is the area that surrounds and covers the basal ganglia. The lower part of the brain refers only to the phys-iological aspects of life, that is, heartbeat, sweat, autonomic func-tions, etc. Today we call it the brainstem. Habits are formed in the basal ganglia of the brain, located in the primitive part of the brain. The unique relationship between different areas of the brain has a significant impact on how we do different things. For example, due to the evolution of the brain, in the layers of activity generated in the new cortex as a result of higher thinking processes, they must go to the brainstem to perform the physical body. It is the brainstem that controls motor activity. However, to pass from the neocortex to the brainstem, the signal must pass through the primary brain. This is where he is kidnapped. For example, the awareness that there is no other drink "on the way" comes from a new skin. It is a conscious decision based on the prognosis of consequences (imagination). But it is kidnapped by the primary brain due to a programmed habit in the basal ganglia of the brain. Since the primary brain has more con-trol over the brain stem than the cortex of the brain, the main brain begins to function.

Another example of this is the manifestation of fear. Fear is also present in the primitive brain. As a centre of habits, it has more control over the brainstem compared to the new rational cortex. The result is a manifestation of fear when the sensitive part of the conscious mind knows that there is nothing to fear. Another example of the duality of our mind can be seen when the new shell creates a terrifying imagination. It is the underlying brain that triggers a response to fear. It is easier to use the example of concern when it comes to habits because the players are the same: the primitive brain and the new cortex. By custom, this mechanism is planted in the primary mind, especially in the basal ganglia. When the further barking of the judges says that the habit is harmful, it seems impotent because they cannot directly control the activity of the body without going through the primitive brain.

NEUROPLASTICITY

Neuroplasticity is a simple phenomenon. Describe the flexibility of the structure of the brain. This structure is not rigid. It can be edited, reversed and edited. The mind at the molecular level creates connections through its axons and dendrites. These neurons have thousands of relationships, and when the memory is encoded in the frontal lobe, it moves through these connections until it connects several relevant minds. For example, if you see a pair of brown shoes that you like, this memory will combine your knowledge of bronze, your idea of footwear, and also combine with all the things you want. It will also connect with everything you saw when you saw this pair of brown shoes. If you saw it in a mall district, the shoe souvenir will also join the mall. With all these connections, it can be quite chaotic. The next time you think of a mall because there is a connection between the two parts of memory, it will also give you an idea for shoes. As there was a desire to buy a pair of shoes, the memory of the shoes also aroused passions.

For an account of reflection and meditation, you will find that the brain is beginning to reform. The power of thinking does not end when you think about things, physically transferring and reconnecting each neuron on a particular subject. Maintains the most appropriate association waves. To do this, cut off unnecessary connections between neurons that should not exist and use the resources released after breaking this link to create new and more meaningful relationships. In this way, the shape of the brain changes. Changes in magnetic resonance imaging (MRI) are detectable and clearer in people who have a lot of reflection and meditation. Thinking is a powerful tool to change the shape and structure of the brain. When the mind is disturbed, seemingly random associations gradually disappear. This is the habit of high-performance people. When random thoughts are rejected, it is easier to concentrate. The most crucial advantage of reflecting and breaking these random associations is that the habits you create are no longer erratic habits that cause strange behaviour. The benefits of reflection in the context of patterns become evident. It helps protect against accidental practices and eliminate bad habits. Neuroplasticity is the reason why we can change our thoughts, beliefs and practices. Neuroplasticity is fueled by meditation and reflection and is the primary tool to rationalize thoughts and actions.

WHY DOES THE BRAIN
NEED HABITS?

The primary method of brain activity is the use of habits. If the structure of the practice is broken in the three-point sequence mentioned above: CAR, then the brain does everything in this sequence. What do you do when the first morning greets you? This answer is found at the end of a short algorithm that is executed in the activation request or a signal. Someone's greeting is a trigger that implements a simple algorithm in which the address is mutual. Otherwise, you may feel uncomfortable. If you answered, it may feel good. This is because when you act, you will receive a reward, even a small one. If no action is taken, a "punishment" (general feeling of discomfort) will be imposed. Both feel in the region of the cortex of the new brain and are arranged from the original mind.

Similarly, everything from bedtime at night, including the use of rituals during the day, such as the way baseball players wear their lucky socks, everything comes from the cycle "when X happens, you do Y". The brain even uses this CAR mechanism. Some are not considered habits. We believe these are the answers. Others are more than patterns, and we call them addictions. This means that these algorithms exist on an aeroplane that flies from a pure reflex to an unsaturated addiction. This brain structure to face the outside world. This is the effect of the causes of the reaction of a person's environment. That is why employers seek individual experience. Experience indicates a previous contact with the event, and the response form no longer exists. There is an algorithm even in sports. Why practice Run Runner beats records: Training allows the mind to create a simple framework to respond to war during the events of everything, from breathing to the contraction of the muscles spreads through them, the transformation of aerobic and anaerobic energy, under certain conditions, be subject habits that occur in these physiological pathways. Patterns require less power to act. Will's activities require much more energy to perform and are less safe (from the brain's perspective) when the result is shown. Habits are predictable. This combined state of predictability and reduced energy makes everything integrated with mental habits a better option. The saying "it is better to choose a demon you know than an angel you don't know" fits perfectly with this internal mental structure. For the same reason, people who fail have difficulty getting up.

It all comes down to habits. The reason why habits become the primary tool of this wheel of the mind is easy to determine. The brain is an excellent resource. The brain weighs 3 pounds, compared to 150 pounds of the body (on average). That is 2% of body weight. However, it consumes 20% of the energy produced by the body's metabolism. Of the 2,500 calories needed to do what we do during the day, 500 calories represent the power of the brain. The mind knows how much energy it needs and, therefore, tries to save as much as possible. Thinking, solving problems, and learning are generally energy-intensive activities. On the contrary, habits are not. The pattern only consumes the power that the body needs to roam and complete the task. There are no mental requirements, and spiritual energy is not necessary for the habit. Because of this, habits become common in the tools used by the body. Imagine you have to think about everything. Should I brush my teeth? What are the benefits? Should I have breakfast? Imagine all those things that are already habits, so think about what would happen if you had to think about it every day and do it without practice. Not only would you spend much energy, but you would also waste your limited time. Energy and time are essential causes in themselves, but this is not the whole story. When something becomes a habit, it disappears in the midbrain: the centre of patterns. The usual algorithms operate at higher speeds than those of the conscious mind. The conscious mind, which is a much smaller area than the whole brain, cannot consider all that is necessary. The reason we can walk and chew gum is that none of them is part of the conscious mind. Imagine having to think with each step, navigate where you are going and activate the large muscles necessary for movement, as well as the small muscles needed for balance; your conscious mind will soon be overwhelmed. Less energy consumption, shorter response time and a better response are the advantages of having the right habits. The perfect golf shot you have seen is muscle memory; it affects your practices when you move until you feel good, finish and reduce the speed of the swing. None of them is conscious because the perfect swing has too many elements that the conscious mind can control. It is a habit exercised by the subconscious. These are the reasons why the brain has patterns. Patterns also exist in other ways. Instead of being a small algorithm or loop, you can also nest them. Patterns can occur inhabits. Think of driving to work on a manual shift. If you follow the same route every day, you can have the conversation you are focusing on, and still, go from point A to point B without paying full attention. You can also stop, move from one gear to the next and navigate, focusing on conscious resources the conversation. Consider how many habits are implemented between them. Thinking about changing gears, the ear increases the engine noise and, when it reaches a specific tone, presses the clutch and changes. You did not have to think about it. It is a habit because you always drive a car. Patterns have a bad reputation because most of the time, we hear patterns in one of two different contexts. First, we believe that we should not have bad habits or, when we are children, tell us that we have bad habits. Second, we are here to practice good habits. It is always a difficult task. Sleeping early should be a good habit, and this is the furthest part of what the child wants to hear. We develop habits combined with negative conclusions. In fact, the more we can move things that are beneficial to our progress, development and results so that they become a habit, the better our lives will be.

HOW TO DEVELOP HEALTHY HABITS, IMPROVE THE QUALITY OF LIFE

He wouldn't worry about trying to adopt new practices unless he took advantage of it. This applies to everything we do in life. We operate on purpose. The fact is that there are many benefits and benefits in the development of positive behavior patterns. You will learn about this in this section. When you finish reading Part I, you will have a clear idea of the lifestyle you can lead when developing good habits. Let's start talking about your stress levels.

UNDER STRESS

S tress is not necessarily bad. It causes our reaction to a fight or flight, which aims to protect us from harm in certain circumstances. Small episodes of short-term stress can save our lives. Anxiety becomes a problem when it lasts a long time. It manifests itself in various unpleasant ways. It affects the way we treat people. If you're like me, you get irritable when you're stressed. It also causes physical side effects such as headache, heartburn, stomach problems and even back pain. Have you ever felt sore when the office or home conditions are chaotic? Stress is probably the cause. Long periods of high pressure can also cause depression, avoid falling asleep and damage the immune system. And if your immune system does not work correctly, you will be more susceptible to disease. There are many ways to deal with stress, from practicing yoga and deep breathing to drinking tea and listening to soft music. The problem is that many people do these things as individual cases or as needed. There is a better approach: identify actions that improve well-being (that is, reduce stress) and transform them into daily habits. For example, suppose you feel overwhelmed with the responsibilities of the office. Do push-ups, squats and squats and see how you feel.

You will probably feel more "alive."This is the result of the activation of endorphins, the reduction of stress and the improvement of mood. Wake up in the morning with a glass of water. This unique habit ensures that you are hydrated, which allows you to control your cortisol levels. (Cortisol is a stress hormone). Adopting good practices can dramatically reduce stress levels. And when you're less stressed, you'll feel better, treat your loved ones better and get a better picture of life. We all have to fight for it!

BETTER APPROACH

Most of us would like to improve our concentration skills. Lack of concentration affects our performance in school and our workplaces. It also negatively affects the relationships we share with our friends and loved ones. If you are a student and have difficulty concentrating, you may be forced to burn oil at midnight, do your homework and prepare for the exams. If you are a CEO, it may be too late to complete tasks that should have been completed that day. The inability to concentrate will also make it difficult to pay attention to your spouse, children and friends when talking to you. There are many exercises you can do to improve your concentration. For example, you can practice storage procedures. But you can also develop your natural concentration skills by adopting specific habits. For example, suppose one of the changes you want to make is more than one. You have enough information on Google. You have had enough of our influential culture that presents messages in small masked fragments as meaningful content. That is why he agrees to read long and informative books or articles every day. It will improve your concentration. You will train your mind to focus on an article or book, instead of getting distracted by an endless stream of fragmented online content. You can also develop the habit of listening carefully. Here you spend time consciously every day when you talk to someone. You would focus on what it says, excluding everything around you. This unique habit will improve your ability to concentrate. Communication with family and famous friends will be an additional benefit. Good habits form the basis of a better approach. And a better approach leads to better performance, stronger relationships and greater efficiency.

HIGHER PERFORMANCE

In the last part, I noticed that improving concentration will increase performance. You know it from experience. Remember the last time you worked in a state of continuous flow, where you paid full attention to the next task. He probably thought it was easy to work without problems and was able to do the job effectively. This is an example of how good habits lead to greater efficiency. Here is another: suppose you learn to wake up an hour earlier each day. Can you imagine how this new routine can affect your productivity? You can probably do more in less time. Or suppose you have a habit of cleaning your desk at the end of each business day. Or check your email twice a day instead of 20 times a day. Or take regular breaks to give your brain a chance to rest. Or set realistic deadlines to complete the tasks. You have an idea. These little habits, all easy to develop and maintain thanks to my 10- step strategy, will help you ignore distractions and do more. The result? You will have more free time to spend with family and friends. You will have more time to devote to your hobbies and passions. You will also like more energy, less stress and better relationships. The best part is that performance increases naturally due to new habits. You can focus on developing a new and healthy lifestyle without paying particular attention to increasing performance. The second is presented as a natural extension of the first. I hope this is an overwhelming advantage.

STRONGER RELATIONSHIPS

The relationships we share with our friends and loved ones determine our overall happiness. Our ability and willingness to create fair connections affect the strength of these relationships. Think about the types of positive habits that support this effort. For example, I said before that listening carefully to someone, or focusing on them, will make a person feel appreciated by you. This feeling opens the door to a deeper level of trust and intimacy. Similarly, consider the positive effect of hugging and kissing your spouse honestly every morning before going to the office. This is a small example of feelings. But now, with signs of love as a frequent victim of our always busy programs, this small screen can have a significant impact on the emotional closeness you share with your spouse. These are just a few examples that show how positive routines (unique activities transformed into habits) can improve your relationship. Here are some other ideas:

Plan 30 minutes of particular time each day with your spouse (no television, no children, no phones, etc.).

Take the time to talk without distracting him.

Congratulate your spouse every day.

Call or visit your parents once a week.

Be encouraging and understanding when your friends share their thoughts with you.

Tell the truth when they ask for your opinion. Friends will appreciate your honesty and trust your sincerity.

These little habits improve the closeness of their relationships. Strengthen trust and deepen the sense of the link. These links are often shown when people experience a lack of listening and lack of attention.

MORE SENSE OF JOY

When we establish and maintain positive and healthy habits, we experience a more satisfying lifestyle. Consider, for example, how low stress, improved concentration, improved performance and stronger relationships can affect your quality of life. You will feel more relaxed, do more in less time and enjoy a more honest and intimate relationship with friends and loved ones. Of course, these benefits are just the tip of the iceberg. There are many others that we will discuss in detail in a moment. The point is that accepting positive behavior creates conditions to enrich your life. Think of the countless ways in which healthy routines can improve your daily experience. You can enjoy better physical and mental health. You can feel full of energy and confidence. You can develop an incredible level of value and self-discipline. To a large extent, their habits and routines also determine their results. Some will help you learn new concepts, develop new skills and think more creatively. Others focus on fitness and can help you lose weight, get fit and feel better. You probably have a list of things you hope to achieve: at home and in your career, in the present and the future. Leaving them to chance is a sure recipe for failure. Instead, create positive procedures that support your goals. When these procedures become part of your life, until you stop thinking about performing them (that is, they will become automatic), you will feel good. The feeling of joy will improve your mood and look at life. They will also help you feel good when you gain more control over the responses to personal and environmental triggers.

BETTER SLEEP QUALITY

If you knew there was a simple way to be more creative, feel more energetic and experience fewer mood swings, would you follow it? What would happen if you could enjoy healthier skin, higher concentration and fewer mistakes during the day? What happens if you get sick less often and feel better every day in business? Begins to seem instructive. The fact is that all are documented effects of good sleep. Experts have long known that the quality of our sleep determines how we feel and how we behave. If you are a student, this affects your ability to learn and get good test results. If you are an entrepreneur, it affects the way you make business decisions. If you are a corporate manager, it affects the way you treat people in a team. If you are a father who stays at home, model how you interact with your children. The good news is that developing positive procedures can help improve sleep quality. For example, suppose you have a habit of doing one or more of the following: going to bed every hour for an hour before turning off the TV one hour before going to bed. Avoid caffeine six hours before bedtime. Listen to the sonata on the piano that he preferred to lie down.

You go to bed at the same time every night. When these habits become part of the nighttime routine, it will be easier to fall asleep. Besides, there is more likely to be more restless and restless sleep. Do these things night after night, and when you wake up, you will feel more rested and full of energy, less stressed and full of energy, healthier and happier. This is the power to incorporate small positive routines in life.

BETTER PHYSICAL HEALTH

Good physical fitness is something we should all strive for. Good health helps us lead a more satisfying life. Staying fit allows us to control our weight more quickly and enjoy better sleep. And, of course, it makes us less sensitive to heart problems, metabolic syndrome and diabetes. When most people think about what it takes to stay fit, they instinctively think about their diet and exercise regimen. Good health is associated with eating healthy foods (and preventing unhealthy foods) and exercising regularly. The problem is that doing these things is difficult. Many of us face a high degree of internal resistance. For example, we want ice cream and French fries, so it is difficult to follow a healthy diet. We prefer to watch the last season of The Walking Dead or House of Cards instead of wearing shoes and going to the gym. What happens if you can improve your physical health by developing small habits that require little time or effort?

Here are some examples: do five push-ups a day. Do five squats a day. Go for a walk 10 minutes and, after waking up, have a glass of water. Reduce food portions by 10%. Remember that none of the above habits is difficult. They don't last long, either. You can do five push-ups in less than 30 seconds. You can do five squats at the same speed. But you will discover that if you do this every day, your physical health will improve. One of my first experiences with small habits appeared in the form of push-ups. This opened my eyes to the effectiveness of starting slowly. He tried to exercise many times in the past. I wanted to force myself to go to the gym, do push-ups and stomach muscles, and even run.

Of course, it never happened. The idea of doing these things was too daunting. Then I committed. I did five pushups a day. No more, no less. I started this new regime that day. In the first week, that was all I did. Five pushups a day. Next week I increased the number to six. I raised it to seven next week. Etcetera Today I do 25 push-ups a day. As a daily reminder, I have created the task many times in Todoist. But to be honest, I don't need it. Performing 25 push-ups is like brushing your teeth. It has become an entrenched habit. I don't feel well until I do them. I cannot (yet) have Adonis' body, but I can distinguish now and when I started. I look better, and I feel better. All this is due to the first day when I decided to do only five push-ups. Later in this activity guide, I will provide more details on how I changed this positive behavior into a daily habit. It will surprise you and delight you with the simplicity of my approach. I am 100% sure it will work for you and me.

ABILITY TO MAKE QUICK DECISIONS

General Patton once said: "A good brutal plan is now better than a perfect plan next week." I have found that this is true in almost all circumstances. But making quick decisions was not natural for me. I overthought everything. That is why I have always made decisions in my personal and professional life. The disadvantage is that I have lost countless opportunities. This affected my relationships with friends and loved ones. This prevented me from doing my job effectively when I was stuck in corporate America. It damaged my productivity as an entrepreneur. In the end, I learned to make decisions quickly. It was a long process. First, I had to commit to change and thus develop new behaviors to support it. That's why I felt comfortable with the rapid decision-making process: I gave myself 60 seconds to make a decision when no more information was needed. When more information was needed, I set a time limit for obtaining it (for example, five minutes). I allowed myself to make bad decisions. And trained to ask: "I think about it too much," he doubted each time. When I was given several options, I immediately eliminated 80%, which made less sense. Like most people, I don't want to disappoint. Then I learned to accept it, if only as a constructive response. By developing these six little habits, I was able to reduce the time it took to make a decision drastically. I'm glad I made an effort. Not only did I discover that making quick decisions leads to more significant opportunities, but making bad decisions rarely has serious consequences. In my experience, overthinking brings few practical benefits.

I am willing to bet that you will discover that it is right in your life. If you tend to overthink things, use the small procedures I described earlier. You will be surprised at the ease with which you can go from overthinking to making quick decisions with short and comfortable habits.

Our lives are so busy, and we are so overwhelmed by our responsibilities in the home and office that creativity may seem forgiving. But experts say that creativity leads to more innovation, better problem-solving skills, less stress and a better mood. In this case, it is worth fighting for more creativity. You probably know someone who says he is not creative. But in a moment we all care. Creativity is like a muscle. He is being taught. More universities than ever offer lessons that guide student's creativity. But you do not have to go to college to develop this muscle. You can do it yourself using small habits. For example, participate in the deepening of exciting topics. Many of us do not. We are used to trusting Google information. We send requests, find the necessary information and move on. We do not make a "deep immersion" in the material that leads to creative thinking. Delving into the details opens the mind and often reveals ideas that would not otherwise arise. The best part is that it is a natural habit. It's just a matter of continually doing it. Sleeping is another small and simple habit that can strengthen creative muscles. By letting the mind wander, the brain can create associations that might otherwise be lost. It presents strange thoughts and ideas that are usually suppressed when tedious tasks are performed. As expected, research has shown that sleep helps people find innovative solutions to severe problems. The point is that you can learn to be more creative and use more creativity. All you need is to adopt small habits.

GREATER CONFIDENCE

Trust is a difficult trait for many people. It is also frustrating because some make it seem so simple. These sociable people, often celebrating, seem to be born with a particular gene of trust. But as with most traits, you can learn to trust. You can exercise enthusiastically to greet people, maintain eye contact and radiate the enthusiasm that attracts people to you. How do you get to the point where your trust encourages others to believe in you? How do you learn to trust your instincts and make decisions with assertiveness and authority? In short, how does trust develop? You do not have to take an expensive course. Nor do you have to spend hours in front of the mirror practicing your speaking style. Greater confidence can result from the development of several simple habits. Here are some ideas: Practice keeping eye contact with Starbucks waiters, local supermarket staff and strangers waiting in line. Improve your outfit. Say hello to a stranger every day. Smile every time you look in the eyes. Identify the small problem and solve it. Whenever you doubt your ability to solve a problem, complete the task or talk, ask yourself why.

In most cases, the reason is emotional rather than logical. Of course, it's just scratching the surface. However, remember that none of the above habits is challenging to develop and maintain. All are small actions you can take for today. This is the central theme of the revolution of little habits: start with a small one to facilitate the immediate start. At first, you may feel uncomfortable, for example, if you are not used to looking people in the eye, but this is the case with learning new behaviors. The good news is that the practice becomes more comfortable. Here is the conclusion: the adoption of small and healthy, essential procedures, which require very little time or effort, can ultimately lead to greater confidence.

MORE EFFORT TO ACHIEVE
YOUR GOALS

It's great to achieve our goals. This behavior fills us with a satisfactory sense of accomplishment. Reaching our goals gives us the confidence that we can reach others and pushes us to take appropriate measures. For example, think about the last time you took steps to lose a few pounds. Didn't you feel good when you looked at the weight and realized that you achieved your goal? Or maybe you wanted to learn to play the piano. Do you remember the sense of accomplishment you felt after becoming an expert? We set goals to improve our lives. This may include weight loss, fitness, learning new skills or investing in the future. Many of us are inspired by the search for a better and more satisfying lifestyle. The challenge is to remain committed to our goals. Determining them is one thing. Another thing is to stay motivated to process them every day. This is the reason why many people abandon their goals. They see a few improvements and some short-term benefits that discourage them from further development. For example, consider losing 25 pounds. Most health experts suggest a slow weight loss at a rate of 2 pounds per week. At this rate, the unit would take almost three months. The goal has been achieved for a long time. It is understood that the person can abandon the purpose that leads to faster satisfaction. There is a much better approach. Depending on the theme of the revolution of small habits, this means adopting minor and easy-to-follow procedures that lead to excellent results. Developing and maintaining simple daily activities changes the purpose of the struggle to achieve the ultimate goal. Eliminate the most significant source of discouragement by reducing the likelihood of abandoning your goals. Instead, it focuses on maintaining healthy habits that ultimately lead to goals. For example, a person who wants to lose 25 pounds will ignore what the weight says every night. Instead, he would concentrate on maintaining the following habits:

Drink a glass of water when you wake up every morning. Simply shop at the edge of the grocery store that shows healthy dishes. (Junk food is usually in intermediate stages). Reduce the size of the food by 10%. Chew the food slowly and taste it. Breakfast, walk 10 minutes every day. Twice a day is better. Eat three meals a day at regular times (for example, breakfast at 7:00, lunch at noon, and dinner at 18:00). Eat healthy and full meals. Examples include almonds, apples and carrot hummus. Maintaining the above habits will help a person who wants to lose weight. Remember that you no longer focus on the number of pounds lost. Instead, the characters in the series are small, healthy and easy to implement procedures. In short: it is easier to stay true to your goals when you focus on the little habits that guide you, not just your goals.

TRIGGERS, PROCEDURES, REWARDS AND LOOPS

Every habit, good or bad, healthy or unhealthy, is triggered by a trigger. When the pattern is fulfilled, it is rewarded or punished. When practices are paid, they become behavior circuits that strengthen over time. It is essential to understand how it works. For the first time, I realized that we would avoid science in the revolution of small habits. Although the brain is so fascinating, spending time studying cognitive psychology has limited practical value. You are reading this activity guide to improving your life. That is why we will focus on real strategies. That said, you cannot enjoy real and lasting success in adopting new habits without at least a theoretical understanding of how these habits develop and maintain. This part of Little Habits Revolution is about triggers, procedures, rewards and loops. We act fast. Drink a glass of water, sit down and hold on tight.

First: definitions

I will introduce a series of terms that you may not know. It is essential to understand them in the context of habit development. Let using four categories that I mentioned at the beginning of the second. For example, suppose you get bored of eating ice cream. Boredom is a factor that triggers a habit in the ice. Routine operation is carried out over and over again. This is another way of referring to a practice or pattern of behavior. We routinely treat it as a unique class. But they consist of a series of actions. For example, consider the habit of eating ice cream. Here is the sequence: stop doing what you do (first action), get up from your chair (second action), approach the freezer (third action), prepare a cup of ice cream (fourth action) and sit for fun (fifth action). Distributing things this way may seem pedestrian. But it reveals what it means to develop a new routine and maintain it. Each step in the series is a potential trap in which the method can collapse. That is why leaving something small, the central theme of the revolution of little habits is such an effective strategy.

Prize

Prizes strengthen procedures. They represent earnings each time you perform an action or a series of actions. In our example of ice cream, the rewards can be sweet taste, creamy texture and delicacy. Or it can be a sense of satisfaction due to the great release of dopamine from sugar consumption. Understanding why we do certain procedures begins with identifying rewards that encourage them.

Tie

The cycle includes three previous ideas. Each behavior cycle consists of a trigger, procedure and reward. This is a key concept to understand. It shows that habits are developed and maintained as a result of stimuli. This is good news because we can control the stimuli to which we are exposed. That is why we have the opportunity to develop every new routine we want. It's about determining the right conditions. As you will see on the following pages, it is easier than you think.

Custom keystone

A key habit is routine, which also affects other routines or behaviors and triggers them. For example, suppose you use the time fragmentation method as a workday strategy. He has discovered that by using a little time, he can concentrate on his work. Less often, you waste time on Facebook, CNN and YouTube. You are also less likely to send text messages to friends, play video games and use the phone application. In this case, using a method of temporary fragmentation is a key habit. Key habits can and should be used to develop new procedures. For example, if you start exercising daily, you are more likely to eat healthy foods. If you wake up an hour earlier each morning, you can drink more water more easily, starting with the first glass after waking up. One habit affects another. These five definitions will help explain the ideas later in this guide. They will be invaluable when we implement my simple 10-step plan to develop new and maintained habits. Let's examine five different types of triggers.

Five different types with trigger

Triggers are probably the most important part of the puzzle. They decide what we do and when we do it. They also affect the degree of strengthening habits in our minds. The continuous use of procedures, the key to their durability, is largely due to the signals that force us to act. In this section, we will discuss five types of triggers. Understanding how they work is invaluable. After understanding them, you can use them to develop and maintain a habit that you believe can enrich your life. Let's start with a trigger that everyone knows, even if they don't recognize it directly.

Weather

Most of us perform certain procedures depending on the weather. For example, when I wake up at 5:30, I brush my teeth, brush my face, use the bathroom, drink a glass of water and get dressed. At 13:00 as dinner. Around 18:00 dinner. Immediately before going to bed, I brush my teeth again. I'm sure you follow similar patterns. Maybe after waking up, would you like coffee? You can enjoy a break to smoke every day at 10:30 or a pinot noir lamp every night at 21:00. Time is one of the most common signs. It is a valuable tool for developing new procedures because it is easy to control.

Location

Many habits are activated depending on the configuration. For example, many of us associate kitchens with food preparation. When we visit this part of our homes, our brains are ready to operate according to this directive. That is why many of us instinctively look for a refrigerator in search of food. Think of signals based on where it operates. Do you want coffee when you get to the office? Do you check your email address at the same time?

Go to school Browse social media while sitting in Starbucks? Like time-based triggers, location-based triggers can easily be used to create new behavior patterns. We will discuss this in more detail in the next section, how triggers and procedures lead to new habits.

State of mind

Our mental state plays an important role in our behavior. How we feel affects our behavior. For example, many people eat when they experience high levels of stress. Many automatically check if they are bored on Facebook and Twitter. Some call the phones to call their friends when they feel happy. Some fall asleep when they feel depressed. The point is that our emotions are a powerful trigger. They urge us to follow learned, healthy or unhealthy procedures. Psychologists say we can control our mental state. This is useful because it means that we can adapt our emotional state to trigger healthy procedures. All you need is to anchor the desired habit to a particular emotion. For example, suppose you want to get into the habit of short walks. The anchor boredom. Whenever you get bored, get up and go for a walk for 10 minutes. Here, emotions are used to indicate the desired routine.

Persons

You've probably heard people describe themselves as drinkers. They rarely drink at home but drink regularly when they are with friends. Their drinking habit is based on the people around them. This type of behavioral response is common. The people we work with are a powerful trigger for many of our procedures. For example, you can smoke with some people in the office during the morning break. You are more likely to train when you meet training partners. You can have a responsible partner that motivates you to do things. Regardless of whether we are aware of it or not, we practice reacting differently to the people in our lives. This is good news: if you can associate or anchor a positive habit with someone in your life, you can use the association as a reliable trigger.

Previous event

As mentioned earlier, many (if not most) of our procedures involve a variety of activities. One action follows another. This action precedes the next, then the next and so on. To illustrate this, think about the process you are going through while preparing to go to bed. You can shower, drink a glass of water, brush your teeth and wear pyjamas. And if you're like me, do these things in the same order every night. This action foreseeably precedes the next. There is a slight difference between the nights. In the context of the development of new habits, this behavior can be used through a strategy called "accumulation of habits". Form new habits by anchoring them in current habits. For example, suppose you want to acquire the habit of threading. Set the tooth brushing activity, previous logical event. Look for dental floss immediately after brushing, which allows your habit to unleash a new habit. Accumulation habits can be used in countless ways to develop positive and healthy routines. We will discuss in more detail in Part VI: How to deliver new habits will last. As you will soon see, this is the perfect approach to develop small habits that grow and resist the passage of time.

HOW TRIGGERS AND PROCEDURES
LEAD TO NEW HABITS

In the previous section, we discussed five different types of triggers (time, position, mental state, people and previous events). We also discuss, at least briefly, how these triggers can be used to create new behavior patterns. In this section, we will discuss more details. This problem is extremely important because it affects your success by adopting new and maintained habits. As we noted earlier, each habit is preceded by a signal. For example, hunger causes a desire to eat. Drowsiness causes a desire to rest. For some, stress causes a desire to smoke or drink. Technically the habits come from the routine. The stimulus (hunger, drowsiness, stress, etc.) leads us to perform procedures or sequences of actions. These activities become a habit when the routine takes root in our minds. Here is a simple example. Let's say you watch the news every night when you go to sleep. The end of the information program acts as a signal. A sequence of activities begins, such as brushing teeth, wearing pyjamas, etc., which ends with lying down and sleeping. Following this routine night after night is deeply rooted in your mind. Over time, it becomes a habit. Think about what this means in the context of developing small and positive habits that improve the quality of your life. If it is possible to anchor the desired behavior pattern to a particular signal, you can develop any imaginable habit. Let me give you an example of how I am currently using this strategy. As you know, I write books that offer detailed plans to increase productivity and design a more satisfying lifestyle. I also have a popular blog (artofproductivity.com). Even if I like to write, I don't always have the motivation. It is a very nice and extremely satisfying job, but it requires a lot of attention and try to do it right.

HOW DO PRIZES STRENGTHEN NEW HABITS?

You already know the use of prizes as a form of positive reinforcement of the desired behavior. We always use them. For example, we use delicacies to encourage our dogs to behave or perform stunts. We use several incentives to encourage our children to get good grades in school. We offer bonuses to our employees to motivate them to achieve specific objectives. The same tactics will help you adopt new and healthy habits. Rewards are part of each behavior cycle. It can be said with certainty that each of our actions is motivated by some kind of reward, regardless of whether we are aware of it or not. We practice looking better. We eat to satisfy hunger. We watch television to relax. We study to get a diploma. We get a job to earn an income. Everything we do, from brushing our teeth to planning a family vacation for the week, is motivated by something we want. In the short term, this desire means satisfying hunger (for example, we eat because we are hungry). In the long run, this means achieving a specific objective (for example, we obtain a university diploma to work in our area of interest). It is important to understand this in the context of habit development because it gives us control. We can choose the awards that are important to us and anchor our new behavior patterns. We receive awards whenever we save the projects. The key to doing this job is to choose prizes that ensure quick satisfaction. For example, suppose you want to train regularly. Getting started is easy. If you ever went to the gym the first week of January, you will see this test. However, maintaining a habit is more difficult. He needs a reward that forces him to act every day. The idea of being fit attracts most people. But this is not a good reward in the context of the development of the habit of exercise. ¿For what? Because adaptation can take months. You need something that offers immediate satisfaction.

Suppose we have a favorite television show. Allow yourself to see this only when you train that day. Or suppose you love naps (if so, you are a person with a heart). Take a 30-minute nap as an exercise reward. Anchoring a new habit in a quick and desirable reward tells the brain that it is worth doing. Not all rewards will be effective for a particular habit. You may have to try to identify the one with the greatest impact. For example, suppose that a 30-minute nap during a nap is not enough to encourage you to train daily. In this case, you will try a different reward and see if it has a greater impact on you. Let's say you like to go to happy hour every afternoon with your friends. Pass the exam. Allow yourself to participate in a happy hour if you train in the morning or during lunch. It is possible that this reward is enough. When you find a reward that motivates you to regular action, use it until it loses its effectiveness. Be consistent, even if the routine is established, the habit has not yet developed. Habits develop through repetition. After all, he doesn't need a reward that encourages him to act. The habit has so many roots that it does so without the need for immediate satisfaction. Depending on your routine, you can start doing it without even thinking about it.

HOW TO CREATE STRONG
HABIT TIES

So far, we have discussed triggers, procedures and rewards, and we have discussed how each of them plays an important role in the development of new behaviors. Let's talk now about how they work together as a system. These elements form a simple 3 step cycle. The first step is the signal. The signal starts the procedure, the second step. Following the routine gives you a prize, the third and last step. The prize at the end of the cycle quenches thirst and gives a sense of satisfaction. Your brain remembers this process and stores it for future use. On the first recognized opportunity, you will try to repeat the process to recreate a positive feeling. When the previously identified signal reappears, the brain will ask you to perform the procedure again. Consider how this natural cognitive process can help you create new and healthy habits that will last. How triggers and procedures lead to new habits, we note that you have the opportunity to choose your signals. Remember my example of using Chopin's prelude in my smallest operation. 28, No. 4 as a signal to start writing. In the section entitled How rewards strengthen new habits, we note that you have the option of choosing your rewards.

And, of course, you can choose the habits you want to be part of your life. In other words, you control every aspect of the habit development cycle. That means you have the key to success. Let's take an example to bring this point home. Suppose you want to get used to reading the facts every night. You must identify the sign and the prize. Suppose you choose night messages as a signal. At the end of the program, turn off the TV and pick up the book. According to the Small Habit Revolution theme, you start with something small. You have read for five minutes.

After reading, enjoy a glass of your favorite Pinot Noir wine. It is your reward for doing the routine. If you go through this process every night, the routine will eventually become a habit. You will find that you want to read nonfiction every night. Over time, you will not need a signal to guide your behavior or a reward that motivates you. The habit will take root in your mind.

REMEMBER THAT YOU
HAVE CONTROL

The most important thing to undo in this part of Little Habits Revolution is that you have total control. You control the whole cycle of habit. Decide to what extent you will adopt and maintain new positive habits in your life. This is exciting news! You don't have to trust anyone to succeed. You also have no circumstances beyond your control. Create your situation. As long as you recognize the right signs and rewards, you can develop all possible habits. Prepare for an experiment to find the one that suits you. The good thing is that you can start building new positive routines that will enrich your life when you're ready. In Part III, we will discuss motivation and willpower, as well as its impact on the development of habits. The facts may surprise you.

Customs and the secret of the will

What is willpower? Willpower is the sword that wields the prefrontal cortex (PFC), the part of the brain directly behind the forehead. For the inexperienced mind, there is a constant struggle between the PFC and the middle brain (main mind). The main mind tries to apply one of its habits after presenting the signal, but the PFC tries to impose a rule or justification that should not be done. Think of the difficulties in making certain decisions, such as the battle between the original brain and the PFC. He is a man who shows the strength of PFC that the midbrain habits have a strong will. It turns out that willpower is simply the ability to resist the pleasure (rewards) that the average brain feeds PFC every time it appears. When PFC tries not to lift a cigarette but opposes chemical addiction and the habit that drives it, the average brain controls the rest of the body in a way that makes life unhappy. But when PFC accepts, it offers an award that makes PFC want this pleasure next time. Many awards weaken the PFC to such an extent that it becomes flexible and inefficient in a wider area of problems. PFC is flexible. The attack of pleasure released by the midbrain can be reduced. To defend yourself, you must be sensitive to the pleasure you feel under the influence of the mind. This way, you can stop your habits. It is also an old and outdated way of doing things. He is considered strong when he manages to overcome the desires of the average brain. It is also easy to rationalize the negative effects of blindly following the pleasures that the average brain feeds on PFC. Simply read Dante's Divine Comedy and other old volumes of philosophy to learn how it works. The secret, however, is that willpower is a temporary and fleeting feature in our mind. It should not be used as a long-term solution, such as inserting a finger into the dam to cover the leak. Willpower is transient. Therefore, willpower alone cannot stop the current that destroys the dam after a while. It usually ends with the person feeling worse. They think that they are not worthy, that they have no discipline and that they are simply weak. Nothing of this is true. The problem is that they trusted the short-term solution as a long-term solution when they had to change their habit. There is a secret to building willpower and its effective use. Use it only as a short-term measure. When he expects his power to survive in the short term, and when time runs out, he discovers that he has more confidence in his willpower. Next time you need it, you will find that it is stronger because it has more trust him. On the contrary, it happens when you demand too much willpower and failure. The next time you trust him, you will see that he is torn. Habits are much stronger than when combined in longer horizons. In the short term, they will explode strongly and can hold the valves until something structural is done to overcome the strength of the habit. Because habits are powerful, as is the Colorado incision in the Grand Canyon, a structural change in habit will produce proportional results throughout life. Food and beverage companies are aware of this and try to encourage younger children to become addicted to their products so they can win in the long term. Caffeine is a sports drink is an example of creating a habit that always works in the background. The way to build willpower is to have a plan. This plan aims to replace willpower after first use and break the habit algorithm. This is a replacement. Each time willpower is used effectively; it is strengthened. When you have a plan and use your willpower to control the initial need to follow a habit and then start the plan, the goal of the will is achieved. This result strengthens the will. Strengthening will helps to overcome the main challenges. Start with something small. Get used to sleeping late. If you decide to wake up at 4:00 and turn on the alarm during this time, all you need is willpower to get up and shower. When the water hits you, you get up. If he sits on the edge of the bed, rationalizing and using his willpower to get up, he will probably fail. On the second day, after using his willpower to get him out of bed to take a shower, he will have more confidence that his willpower will work. On the second day, you have more confidence and do the same. Now you are beginning to believe that you have goodwill. Now you can face seemingly clearer challenges. In this illustration, the plan was to take a shower. His willpower consisted only of feeding this part of the whole. After bathing, he now has something stronger than getting up. A year later, after getting up at 4:00, he realizes that he has a better life and has achieved more. Because of this, you have more confidence in your willpower to wake up at 4. It was a plan combined with the willpower that brought you there.

HABITS THAT MAKE A DIFFERENCE

Success in any field is a consequence of the action. It is impossible to obtain the knowledge, skills and credentials necessary to reach the top of the stairs simply by sitting and contemplating throughout the day. Common wisdom recommends putting on and sustaining the tumult and muscles. This is good advice, but it is also the reason why many people give up and choose a simpler life. There is nothing wrong with choosing a simpler life if you do it for the right reasons. If you choose a simpler life because you have no will and you intend to do something for life, then you are late. You didn't make that decision; you decided something easy. There is a better way: habits are an important characteristic of the human psyche. These are forces with which you cannot fight. But you can change them. Changing habits is a topic that will be discussed in the next chapter. The question we face is: why change them? Five strong habits are strong enough to change a person's trajectory: the power to refrain from judging; Positive power to distil all events; the power of authenticity; the power of curiosity; and the power to take responsibility. It should be noted that this is not a list of habits that say you wake up early, exercise or eat well. They can also be habits. This specific list is designed to attack the core of your habits centre and eliminate various existing habits and transfer them through those that will have the greatest impact on many other areas of your life. Think of it this way, the fastest way to turn off all the lights in the area is not to go to each house and turn off individual objects, but to go to the substation and turn it off. These five habits are designed to make key changes that will affect the areas that lead to a higher standard of living.

Verdict

The tendency to judge is a deeply rooted habit in most of us. Every time we see someone doing something different from what we do, or it is contrary to our programming, we dedicate time and effort to judge the whole person according to the unique thread shown at that time. Judgment is at the centre of many qualities and prevents us from seeing the good that comes from many possibilities. This habit is formed at a very young age. It is the core of many other shadows in us, including prejudice, racism, prejudice, etc. We judge because it is a habit. There is no other reason why we have a habit because classification classifies things and is designed to give us security. If we see someone walking at night, fear is based on the habit of fearing the unknown. We prefer to be careful because it keeps us safe. It also prevents us from taking risks and improving our lives.

Negativism

It's hard to be positive about things when we have a habit of being negative. The habit of being negative results from the need for caution. The body develops certain qualities over time, and because it tries to use as little energy as possible to rethink everything several times, it reaches a general conclusion. "Prevention is better than cure," says the saying. In this case, it is better to be negative than positive. It is better to be pessimistic than optimistic. But these impressions and possible habits are errors that control most of our actions.

Negativism can provide security in several areas, but it also becomes a barrier to learning and a barrier to seizing opportunities. Finally, negativity is a habit and must be replaced. Positivism is the habit you are looking for, and it is a proven habit of the most successful people. Positivism is the main principle of all successful people. They will never make an effort without him. Negativism dictates that what they accept will fail and they may conclude that it is better not to try.

Plagiarism

Plagiarism is not just copying a classmate's homework. It is a mentality that presents nothing new. The copy is rooted directly in the middle of the brain. The mind wants to achieve but does not want to spend the energy necessary for creativity and original thinking. To find what has already happened and imitate it. It is a habit that can be overcome and is one of the habits of successful people: originality and authenticity.

Modelling someone and doing something that has worked best is not plagiarism. The problem is to copy what they have done and pretend that it is yours. It is not only about the robbery of the creator that suits him but about cultivating a habit that will ruin him in the future. It should not only be original but also fight for authenticity. We can all do something that another person cannot do. We may not find it. If we decide to accept this false person, we miss the opportunity to be what we are best suited to. Anarchy is a habit. Being a follower is a habit. You will never find an observer above. Observers, by definition, remain below as stated above.

Apathy

We are so engrossed in the curiosity that it killed the cat that we decided to be indifferent. We choose to limit our curiosity to what others do on social channels. Indifference is a habit that must be eliminated. After the abolition of indifference, many areas of life will come to light.

Irresponsibility

Irresponsibility is also a habit. It is a habit that grows in other areas and causes loss of self-esteem. Responsibility is the main characteristic of true leaders. If Gandhi were not responsible for the situation he saw, India would not be released. If Martin Luther King was not responsible for the rights of all people, there would be no progress in civil rights in the United States. Taking responsibility is the main mentality and habit of successful people. On the contrary, it turns out that irresponsibility and the practice of apathy are the nature of those who never really succeed. Here are five habits to try, and they are a great start. The goal is always to start small. Never try to bite more than you can chew. Bite and gradually increase what you can change. You will finally get there. The people at the top who have all these habits did not get there as soon as they left kindergarten. They also had to work on it.

THE FIVE HABITS THAT ARE AT THE CENTRE OF YOUR BEING ARE THOSE THAT NEED TO BE CHANGED TO HAVE MAXIMUM IMPACT

It is not enough to know that you can change your habits. Disappointment for losing consciousness about changing bad habits. If you want to succeed, first change these five habits. From there, he will begin to discover that habits with less influence are revealed. From there you can also change them. Of course, getting up at 4 in the morning is a good habit, but it does not appear in these five habits, because when you change the apathy and irresponsibility mentioned above, you will notice that you want to get up early to do more things. You don't need the willpower to do it when you have a reason. To counteract the five existing bad habits, you must change them to the following five good habits:

Understand

Positivism

Originality

Passion

Responsibility

Understand

Instead of wasting time and effort judging someone who makes a mistake, successful people are aware of the mistake and wonder how to learn from it. Others make the best mistakes, but they can be learned. That's why we are always looking for a biography to see how others solve the same problems we face. We don't copy them, but we try to find among those we read. Develop the habit of understanding, and you will see that you are in a better mood, that you have more confidence to publish your work and that you can learn more from others. All of this will accelerate your progress.

Positivism

Positivism is not just a mentality; it is a habit. For example, you cannot control your anger if you have the habit of anger. The force of habit (anger) is too powerful to try to use willpower to avoid anger. Similarly, you cannot control negative willpower; you must be positive. When you have the habit of positivism, it comes with great strength. Developing positivism and allowing it to be activated in the most difficult situations will give you a strong personality and strength to face the challenges.

Originality

To reach the top, you must be able to provide something that others do not. This is from the original definition. Most Fortune 500 companies were created in search of original ideas. From Ford to Apple and Google, the ideas used by the individual founders were original and effective. Their innate originality allowed them to improve the situation, see everything more clearly and go further to succeed. The desire to be original is a habit. The vision of originality will not be strong enough to face the challenges.

Passion

Bad, but easy, this passion is a lonely feeling. We are passionate about one thing, but not the other. We know that what we achieve in life generally fascinates us. But what exactly is passion? Passion is a cauldron of indestructible fire that burns when it sees something fruitful or materializes in your hand. When passion becomes a central habit, it becomes unstoppable. Passion burns and tends to burn all obstacles on the ground. Responsibility generally does not correspond to the visceral definition of a habit. We always think of habits such as morning coffee or smoking after a meal. These are not habits we want to change. This will happen, of course, after a successful change of central programming in your habits centre. When you can change these five traits in a habit that is activated by certain signals, you will see that success occurs effortlessly. The responsibility is one of them.

Responsibility, regardless of whether it is your children, pet, product or even what you say or how you say it, allows you to expand your field of influence. Responsibility is the strength you leave when you take care of everything you find. Modern language speaks of that. When you get used to "owning", there is no situation that cannot be overcome. The five existing habits listed above and the five habits you want to have are interrelated. To counteract apathy, replace it with passion. To counter this process, replace it with understanding. The next chapter will show you how to do it in just thirty days.

MOTIVATION VS. WILLPOWER

W hat determines your success? When we think about developing good habits, we instinctively assume that it requires motivation and willpower. We believe we need something wonderful that inspires us and makes us act now. And when we operate, we understand that maintaining good habits is a matter of determination. Many of us grew up in this. What would happen if our hypotheses about the development of habits were completely wrong? What would happen if we were persuaded of the role of motivation and willpower in creating new procedures? What if they are not the key to success? That would explain why so many people, including motivated and determined, don't have good habits. In Part III of the Little Habits Revolution, the double role of motivation and willpower will be explored. You will learn why no one will agree with the effectiveness of a small habit that will take root and grow slowly over time.

Because motivation is not enough

"I have no motivation." How many times have you heard this answer when you ask people why they have not taken action? It is as if our ability to act depends entirely on whether we are inspired to do so. The right motivation can lead us to action. For example, even if we are weak, we will be motivated to run if the lion chases us. The problem with motivation is that it is always short-lived. It never lasts; it means that it is an extremely inefficient tool to develop and maintain new habits. The increasing amount of scientific evidence suggests that the elements that motivate us to act may have the opposite effect. Let's take the example of using prizes.

As you know, rewards can be a powerful motivator. But psychologists have discovered that they can demotivate us. A study published in the Journal of Personality and Social Psychology in 1973 analyzed the impact of numerous awards on children encouraged to draw. The authors said that when the prize was expected, children spent less time drawing than more. Other studies have shown similar results. The analysis of 92 studies that analyze the impact of cash prizes on the results of the work showed that there was practically no correlation between these two elements. (The results are described in the Journal of Vocational Behavior in 2010) Why is motivation not a reliable indicator of consistent action? There are several reasons: first, it is unstable. Down and nothing. BJ Fogg, the founder of the Stanford Persuasive Technology Laboratory, describes this "wave of motivation." Motivation levels rise and fall, which makes them an incredible tool for designing new behaviors. The second reason is that it is unpredictable. There is no way to predict when you will feel motivated, and when you will feel motivated.

Therefore, you cannot rely on motivation to encourage him to act (that is, observe the desired habit).

Third, as I said before, the motivation is short-lived. While useful for encouraging immediate action, it does not encourage repetition. Many of us feel motivated as a stream of emotions. It happens in a short time. Rarely, if ever, we experience the same thing day after day. Fourth, motivation often depends on our internal communication. For example, suppose your boss asks you to do something that seems inappropriate. It is difficult to motivate yourself if the fact is incompatible with your values and beliefs. Or suppose you have a habit of telling him that he must "train." What comes first when you feel you have to do something? Resistance The resistance inside is enemy motivation. Both are like oil and water. They cannot occupy the same space. When resistance raises its head, motivation tends to fade. You cannot trust that it will help you develop new behavioral models that require continuous action over time. These are the reasons why motivation is never enough to create and maintain new and healthy procedures. You can encourage us to do unpleasant things, such as fees or visits to the dentist. However, it is an ineffective tool that inspires daily activities. If motivation is not the answer, what about willpower? Do you offer a solution to create lasting habits? Let's see in the next section.

IS WILLPOWER THE SOLUTION?

If motivation inspires us to act (even sporadically and involuntarily), what encourages us to do so? Many people say that the answer is willpower. They claim that with sufficient determination and courage, we can force ourselves to do things that we would not otherwise do. This is true to some extent. If we strive to achieve a particular result, we can force ourselves to act to achieve that result. For example, suppose you are determined to run a mile for exercise. You can have enough willpower to put on your shoes and go to the track. The question is: will you have enough willpower to do it tomorrow, the next day and the next day? Can you count on the personal determination to create and maintain this new habit? The answer is no. There are two reasons: first, scientists have discovered that willpower is a limited resource. It ends with time. We will discuss this idea later, entitled the problem with force of will. Second, willpower is short-lived. It is like a Roman candle; initially, it burns but disappears quickly. This feature makes it a useful tool to resist instant temptations, for example, eating ice cream on a diet. However, it is less useful for developing new behavioral models that require a consistent application, preferably daily. In the next part, we will discuss willpower issues. You will learn why determination alone is not enough to create lasting procedures. This is a key problem because many people think that lack of willpower is the reason they fail when they try to develop good habits. The truth is much simpler. This is the solution, but I am ahead of me. First, let's bury the idea once and for all, that willpower is the key to creating positive and healthy habits.

The problem with the strength of will

In the previous section, I noticed that there were two main problems with willpower as a tool for developing habits. First, this is a limited resource. Second, its usefulness is limited to a short period. Let's talk in detail about these two deficiencies. In 2011, Proceedings of the National Academy of Sciences (PNAS) published a fascinating study. Strange factors have been titled in court sentences. The authors tried to find out why the judges' decisions were generally favorable for prisoners in the morning and less favorable later. To present their study, they noted that "we tested the comic book of universal realism, that justice was" what the judge ate for breakfast. "The authors investigated more than 1,100 bankruptcies in a period of 10 months. They discovered that the judges were more capable of condemning prisoners at the beginning of the business day and immediately after lunch, but as the day and decision sessions passed, the judges began to issue less favorable decisions under legal circumstances. Similar scientists attributed the effect of "exhaustion mental." They believed that judges felt fatigued in making decisions, and the data indicated that they were getting worse with each failure. The study shows the greatest lack of willpower in the context of development. Habits: This is a limited resource, it's like a full tank of gas in a car, start the day with you for a constant reserve and willpower, but every decision you make recipe in it at the end of the day, there is no willpower or not, which makes it difficult to resist temptations in the short term. For example, suppose you want to get used to running. If you commit to doing this as your first action every morning, you will probably have the necessary willpower. Assuming a good night's sleep, start the day with the "fuel tank." But what if you run after work? This can be problematic unless the habit is already part of your daily schedule.

Everyone will use some of their willpower, leaving them seriously exhausted. As you can see in the study that evaluates judicial decisions, fatigue is caused by fatigue of decisions. There was minimum willpower left in the tank because you used it to make decisions throughout the day. Therefore, it will be more susceptible to short-term temptations. For example, you are more likely to give up the desire to relax on the couch and watch TV instead of running. The fact that willpower is a limited resource that is running out is a relative discovery. However, this has far-reaching implications for its usefulness (or lack thereof) in the creation of long-term behavioral procedures. The second great lack of willpower is that it is only useful in the short term. Remember that the creation and maintenance of a new routine, regardless of this, if you are flossing, reading non-fiction or doing push-ups, require continuous use. Regular exercise is necessary to maintain the routine. The problem is that, as mentioned earlier, willpower burns first but disappears quickly. That means you can't trust him. Your reserve of willpower will often be empty, which exposes you to temptations that go beyond efforts to develop new habits. This is one of the most common reasons why many people find it difficult to develop new and lasting behavior patterns. New behaviors are easy to create but almost impossible to maintain only with willpower. Unfortunately, many people trust him without realizing his limited nature, easy to use and in the short term. As a result, they involuntarily sabotage their efforts from the beginning. In the next chapter, why habits always triumph over willpower, I will describe the easiest and most effective way to maintain new procedures.

Because habits always succeed at willpower

If neither motivation nor willpower helps you create and maintain new behavior patterns, what is the solution? It's simple: little habits. As we noted in Part II: Triggers, procedures, rewards and loops, it triggers fast behaviors that result in rewards. These are the rings. But the behaviors or procedures in these circuits are not yet habits. Transforming them into habits requires constant use. As we have already discussed, the motivation is temporary and fleeting. He comes and goes, so you can't trust him. Willpower is an expression of self-control. When we decide something (cut, run, etc.), we must resist the temptation to do more attractive things (watch TV, take a nap, etc.). Remember, however, that willpower is a limited resource that runs out from the moment we wake up in the morning. Therefore, like motivation, you cannot count on it. But think about what will happen when you make a habit. Become an integral part of everyday experience, often to the point of doing it without thinking. Do not compare this with other options. Nor is there an internal debate about whether he has enough energy to create a habit. It is part of your life, and you follow it. For example, you brush your teeth every morning. Don't think about it; just do it? It is a deeply rooted habit and part of everyday experience. You don't have to be motivated to brush your teeth. You also don't have to practice willpower. It is simply done. This applies to all developed habits, from the buckle of the seat belt when getting into the vehicle, to typing without looking at the keyboard. Do these things without thinking. They are rooted in your mind. Therefore, habits, even the smallest ones, will always have priority over willpower and motivation when maintaining new procedures. Over time, they take root so deeply that you feel uncomfortable when you neglect them.

For example, try to remember the last time you left home after forgetting to brush your teeth. He probably felt restless, even if he didn't know the cause immediately. This is the strength of habits. Once created, they are indestructible. In Part IV: 10 steps to model healthy habits that will last, I will give you a simple and detailed plan to develop every habit you can imagine. Here the wheels meet.

HOW TO CHANGE YOUR HABITS
IN JUST 30 DAYS

If you do it right, it will be less than thirty days to abandon a series of habits and enter another. In some cases, you will use willpower to help you, but you must remember that the goal is to eliminate habits in the middle of the brain and replace them with the habits you want. The exchange from within will change the various connected areas and affect an important part of your life. The body was not designed to eliminate the habit and leave the resulting cavity empty. It never works and can cause depression in some people. The best way is to replace a habit that has been eliminated by another habit. Think about what nicotine patches do when someone tries to quit smoking. The patch replaces the nicotine obtained from the cigarette. The key to changing your old habit is to find a new one and transfer the old one to the new one. Many people think that they must get rid of the old in a separate movement before vaccinating the new. Not only is this more difficult, but it is a shock to the system and requires a strong will to prove its worth. It also has a better chance of failure. For example, if you are trying to eliminate sugar from your diet, you can replace it with Sweet's Low and then with something else, such as Stevia, until everything goes out of your system. Move with you to eliminate the five old habits, in the last chapter, use five new habits to transfer them accordingly. So, as we said before, the way it works is to deny judgment with understanding, negativity with positivism, and plagiarism with originality, apathy with passion and irresponsibility with responsibility. The result will be nothing innovative. Displacement strategy Now that we know how to apply the displacement and have determined what to eliminate, the displacement method remains. Remember that this should be done in small portions. Change your habits in small steps. Have you ever had a song stuck in your head? The best way to get rid of it is to listen to another song. After some repetitions, the first song will be deleted from the repeat mode. The first key to changing habits is to identify triggers. You may not have control over the triggers, but you do have control over what your mind wants to do in response to a trigger. To find the act that needs to be changed, you must think carefully about what you must do to get a positive result.

Situation. If the waitress takes the wrong order instead of judging it, she looks at the trigger and realizes that her mistakes disturb her. So take the mistakes that bother you and take the action you will take the next time the signal begins. Think about how you behave. You can find a solution in your reflection. When you find a solution for another action, divide it into small pieces. Instead of judging, the next time someone makes a mistake, take the action you thought. You will begin to feel better about yourself. The change is not static, especially for the five new habits that you try to instil to replace the previous five — being static means that new statistics are the ultimate goal. If you choose a nicotine patch to quit smoking, you will not spend the rest of your life using it. Eventually, it will also eliminate it.

Similarly, not only try to find a change of judgment in something else but follow a path that leads to someone's mistakes as a reason to understand, not to judge. The change between judging and showing understanding is not fast. Choose the path you are getting used to for the first time with the habit of something else. If you have a habit of eating, instead of trying to change your habit to go from overeating directly to a seven-day fast, you can start by changing the food you eat. Instead of the candy you ate, turn them into cereal bars, then turn them into Rice Krispies, then carrot sticks and then celery. See how gradual the change is. Change from a more offensive habit to habits that are not so bad, so stay tuned until you need the habit. The five habits that should be part of each person's personality are ideal for changing the path of their lives. To get there, it must be done in several stages. The steps should be designed according to your personality and how you perceive yourself. At the same time, if you do not feel that you want to deal with the cardinal habits of your life and change them immediately, then it is understandable. You must do what you think you can achieve without stress.

REFLECTION AND TRIGGER

Displacement As we have said, a great tool to look for old habits and replace them with new ones are reflexes. Reflection does many things and is one of the things that people do with great success. When you think you change things and look at yourself. It is a way of taking responsibility for everything. This is not a session where you blame yourself for everything, but see where you can make a positive difference for everyone and everything around you. The reflection allows you to see things as they are. If you know, that criticality is not a good feature, and now you know that you should change it.

Understanding and reflection will allow you to see the steps you should follow in your life. Take you from where you are to where you should be. For example, if you want to create a new reading habit, and the habit you have now should seem compulsive. You can decide to move to the last one. One of the most important things you know about this and the previous chapter is that you can't do it with a big jump. You must break it down. In your reflection, find the triggers of compulsive observation. Do you lift your feet after a hard day at the end of the day? Are you in bed before bedtime? Whatever it is, there is an activation mechanism that leads to this state. Find this trigger. After identifying the trigger, you now have a focal point that you can avoid. You can avoid compulsive observations every night, regardless of whether you decide to read some pages of an interesting book, go to dinner, spend time at a friend's house, go to the gym and even take a mini-vacation for a long weekend. When he returns home next week, he will stop watching television or his favorite device. If you pulled the trigger or moved everything together, you will discover that it is not difficult to avoid it.

Change the prize

In one of the examples above, when you go to the gym, you do two things. First, you avoided the trigger to go home and stretch on the couch. This whole scene is a trigger. When you stop the trigger, the pulse will not increase. Then, when you give yourself another reward, break the habit you have created for the habit you are trying to break. Whether you pull the trigger, the reward or both, you will find that it eliminates the momentum and motivation to act. Thanks to this, the habit is already breaking, and soon it is breaking. Now he has three movement strategies in his arsenal. There is a general change in habits in which one habit replaces another. It has a trigger change in which it completely avoids the trigger, and then it has a rewarding change in which it presses an alternative act: do something more enjoyable than the previous one. If you are addicted to chocolate, you can change the chocolates for thirty days and go to the other side without wanting chocolate. At the moment he has two supports: where he is now (still thirsty for sweets) and where he wants to be in thirty days without hunger. The full-screen period is the key to the entire process. Having intermediate steps satisfies the need to move slowly inhabits.

TEN STEPS TO MODEL LONG-TERM
HEALTHY HABITS!

This is the material you were waiting for. The details that precede this point determine the stage of the habit development plan that I will present to you. Your knowledge of the triggers, procedures, rewards, motivations and willpower will be essential for your success in adopting and maintaining new habits. I organized this plan in 10 steps to make each step easy to apply. Each step is simple but necessary for the plan to work. Skip one and run the risk of sabotaging your efforts. Read Part IV in its entirety. Then review the necessary steps to get inspired or remember why they are important. In this way, you will benefit: this simple 10-step plan will help you develop the positive habits you want. Do you want to start training? This is how you do it. Do you want to start reading nonfiction books? This plan will show you how to do it. Do you want to start eating better and drinking more water? You are about to learn a safe strategy. Do you want to increase your productivity, be more organized, save more money or be more sociable? This 10-step plan is the answer. As you will see on the following pages, creating a new and lasting behavior is a safe strategy.

1: Explain the goal you want to achieve with the new habit

Before rushing to develop a new habit, it is important to know why you want to do it. As I mentioned in Part I: How to develop healthy habits, improve the quality of life, we operate with a goal. We do things for some reasons, even if we don't think about it. For example, we brush our teeth every day by habit. We do this to keep them clean, prevent tooth decay and freshen breath. These results are our goal. The same applies to all our activities, from exercise and diet to organizing desks and cleaning the kitchen. We operate on purpose. We act with intention. With this in mind, first, determine the specific result you want to enjoy. What you want to achieve let's say you want to lose 20 kilos. Weight loss is simply a means to an end (or perhaps many goals). In particular, you want to enjoy more energy during the day, look thinner, feel better and protect yourself against heart disease. These are the desired results. They inform you about the types of habits you will follow. Many people try to develop new behavior patterns, without paying attention to the specific objectives they want to achieve through them. They often have little more than a vague idea. For example, they may want to "take shape" or "be healthier." But its objectives are not specific. Therefore, they rush to adopt habits that are not suitable for them. Could you do it better? Before choosing the habits you want to apply, discover what you want to achieve after the party. Be specific; for example, don't say you want to lose weight. Determine the number of pounds you want to lose, as well as the reasons why you want to lose them. After obtaining the desired result, go to step 2, making sure to choose the habits that best complement it.

Step 2: Determine the custom you want to develop

After explaining the objective, you can choose with confidence the habits that will accelerate the process to achieve it. You will not risk choosing new behaviors that will delay the process or, worse, completely derail your efforts. Let's say, for example, that we want to lose weight. As noted in the previous section, this is a vague objective that requires clarification. Why do you want to lose weight? What do you hope to achieve by doing this? Let's also assume that you decide to skip step 1. Instead, immediately choose a habit that you think will help you lose extra pounds. The problem is that you can choose a habit that helps you lose weight but sabotage your long-term goal; for example, you feel better or have more energy. Many weight-loss strategies can harm your long-term health and affect your well-being. The good news is that if you did step 1, you have already explained your goal. You know exactly what you want to achieve. Choosing a new habit, and especially the right habit of achieving it becomes a child's play. Using our example of weight loss, suppose your goal is to enjoy more energy in the afternoon, at this time of day, when mental fatigue usually occurs. Here are some small habits that can help:

Lie down 30 minutes before each night.

Eat a light lunch.

Avoid sweet snacks.

Choose snacks with protein.

Perform five push-ups during each afternoon break.

Stay hydrated

Reduce the number of afternoon work sessions to 30 minutes. Take a 5-minute break between them. Stretch your muscles or go for a walk. Keep in mind that some of these habits are not directly related to weight loss. Instead, they relate to your main purpose, the reason you want to lose weight. They help maintain energy levels and prevent afternoon depression. As an additional benefit, they will also help you lose extra pounds. This example shows how important it is to explain an objective before choosing a new habit. Thanks to this, you can choose the right habit for the job. In step 3, we will analyze how to ensure that you perform the new procedure regularly.

Step 3: Breaking a new habit to the minimum of iteration

The biggest obstacle to creating a new habit is that we often discourage it. It takes a lot of effort to realize that we feel discouraged. For example, in the past, I have tried to do push-ups as a form of daily exercise many times. I still failed. My problem was that I was referring to a "reasonable" number of push-ups that would help me recover. There were 50 of them. He hasn't gotten in years. Execution 10 in a row required the suspension of disbelief, let alone 50. I tried to defend it. It was not sweet. My hands moved uncontrollably after the seventh shift. In order, I gave up. Not once not twice many times. I thought that if I couldn't do ten push-ups, what would happen? This perspective was completely wrong.

My problem was not that I couldn't do more than a few laps. My problem was that he didn't let me start at an early age. A small beginning eliminates resistance. Eliminate discouragement and encourage action. In Part I: How to develop healthy habits improves the quality of life, I said that I now do 25 push-ups a day. I did not say that they are relatively easy at this time. Here is the key: I didn't start with 25.

I allowed myself to start small, doing only five push-ups a day. I increased the number in increments of one each week. This eliminated any excuse that should be executed. I could do five push-ups, even if I saw them shrink. And most importantly, he didn't need willpower or motivation. I had to start with something small. Leo Babauta, who runs the popular ZenHabits.net website, once said about adopting new habits: "Make it easy not to refuse."

In other words, divide your new habit into the smallest iteration. If you are trying to do push-ups, start with five (or even one). If you want to drink more water, start with an extra ounce. If you are trying to get up early, set the alarm five minutes before the time you usually get up. Let yourself start at an early age. You will find that thanks to this, you will eliminate any internal resistance that you will feel at the beginning. Next: choose a reliable signal that encourages you to impose a new habit.

Step 4: create a signal to activate the habit

As I said in the section entitled Triggers and procedures lead to new habits (see Part II), triggers (or signals) precede all learned behaviors, at least at the beginning. The most important thing to remember is that we review them. We establish the circumstances that lead us to action. For example, if you want to start running every morning, you can put running shoes next to your bed. Seeing them after waking up would be a trigger that would allow you to run. If you want to keep your workplace clean, you can clean it every day before leaving the office. In this case, the trigger is at 5 pm (or every time you leave the office). I said I use Chopin's prelude in my minor surgery. 28, No. 4 as a writing trigger. I listen to this chapter. I arrived at my local cafe 20 minutes ago, went to my Macbook and immediately went to work. Identify the action or sequence of actions that can act as a trigger for your new habit. Research suggests that the best approach is to choose an existing routine that points to a new one. In 2011, the journal Psychology, Health & Medicine published a study that analyzed several approaches to modelling and maintaining new habits. The authors stated that the combination of new and existing habits proved to be the most effective way. They noted that "new behaviors were often incorporated into existing procedures, and their predictability, stability and order particularly favored the integration of new behaviors." Think of a new habit you want to model. What are you currently doing with a ritual that can act as a trigger? For example, suppose you want to start short walks every day (a good form of low impact exercise). Meals can serve as triggers; when you finish eating, walk 10 minutes. Or you can use time as a trigger (although experts are divided as to its effectiveness). You can schedule walks at 10:00, 12:30, 16:00 and 19:00. If you want to floss daily, use a toothbrush as a trigger.

The signals you choose will help you overcome the inevitable internal resistance you will experience as you form new habits. When you are tired, motivated and have no willpower other than sitting on the couch and watching TV, you will be encouraged to act. If you don't have a procedure that you can use to indicate a new habit, create it. Although this is less effective than using an existing procedure, this is another better option. Take advantage of time, position and even emotional state. For example, suppose you want to get into the habit of greeting strangers. You may not have an existing procedure that can trigger this behavior. But you can create one based on your location. Here's how: Commit to welcoming at least one stranger every time you visit a local supermarket. Or promise yourself that you will receive a stranger in the Starbucks line. Over time, this position- the based procedure will automatically detect a new habit. In the next part, we will discuss how to create a progressive plan for a new habit.

Step 5: Set a clear goal

This step is simple. However, this is one of the most important steps in the process of defining habits. Step 6 depends entirely on him. Here you assign a numerical value to your new habit. This value will help you develop a habit development plan and allow you to track your progress along the way. Let me explain ... Suppose you want to start doing push-ups. As we noted in step 3, you should start with something small. Do not start with the 50th goal per day if you are addicted to television (I am speaking from experience). Instead, start with five. You can do five. Your arms may shake a little, but you will not die. Five is the numerical value of this new habit. It gives you a starting point in stone. Check if you managed to create a new habit on a specific day. If you do three push-ups, you will know that you will have to do two more before you can request success. It seems simple and maybe even for pedestrians. However, this is a key step towards creating behavioral patterns that persist when faced with obstacles. You need a number that defines your daily success. Here are some examples of taking this point home:

A new habit: greet strangers.

Numerical value: greet three strangers every day.

A new habit: meditation.

Numerical value: meditate for 60 seconds every morning.

A new habit: write a personal diary.

Numerical value: write for five minutes every night.

You have an idea, and numbers define success. There is no ambiguity. Specify when the habit of the day ended successfully. Next: we will create a plan to expand your new habit.

Step 6: Designing with a plan slowly increases your new habit

Some habits are everyday and unique. He is not interested in increasing the number of repetitions. He just wants to make sure he does it every day. An example is flossing. You should make sure that it happens every morning or afternoon (or both). He is not interested in doing this 20 times a day. Other habits are excellent for increasing the number of repetitions or the time spent on them each day. Here are some examples:

Lizards
Drinking water
Go for a walk
Nonfiction Reading
Enter potential customers
Connect with potential customers

To write a diary

To meditate

Greetings to strangers

Do not assume that the habit increases naturally over time. Create a plan to do this. Otherwise, internal resistance and external obstacles will disturb you. For example, let's use our pump example from the previous section. You will remember that we start with five push-ups a day. This problem, our daily goal,

Let's say you want to do 50 pushups a day. Here is a hypothetical plan that will help you work to this point:

Week 1: do five push-ups

Week 2: do eight push-ups

Week 3: do 11 push-ups

Week 4: do 14 push-ups

Week 5: do 17 push-ups

 Week 6: do 20 push-ups

Week 7: doing 23 push-ups

Week 8: doing 26 push-ups

Week 9: doing 29 push-ups

Week 10: doing 32 push-ups

Week 11: doing 35 push-ups

Week 12: doing 38 push-ups

 Week 13: doing 41 push-ups

Week 14: doing 44 push-ups

Week 15: doing 47 push-ups

Week 16: up to 50 push-ups Sixteen weeks.

Four months Achieving the goal may seem like a long time (50 push-ups per day), but the weeks pass quickly. At the end of the fourth month, you will look back and be surprised by the progress. It is important to create a solid plan to achieve your goal. Without a plan, you will have to rely on your motivation, willpower and mood to increase your new habit. It prepares you for failure. You will notice that the gradual increase in our hypothetical plan is small. We increase the number of push-ups only three times per week. This approach is according to the main theme of the revolution of small habits. Starting small and gradually earns the day. In the next section, we will create a reward system that will inspire you to maintain a long-term habit.

Step 7: Create a SIMPLE award system

You will remember in the section how rewards strengthen new habits that positive reinforcement plays an important role in the development of habits. As I have noticed, everything we do is motivated by the type of reward received immediately (for example, praise) or in the future (for example, promotion). Rewards are a powerful tool for developing new behaviors. The more positive they are, the more they inspire us to act. That is why it is worth creating a reward system that will help you develop the new habits you choose. How do you choose a reward that inspires and does not sabotage your efforts? First, reduce it. Suppose you have a habit of cleaning your desk at the end of each business day. Don't reward yourself with an expensive dinner next to your favorite grill. Instead, enjoy your favorite chocolate bar (choose a smaller "fun size" if your weight is concerned). Research shows that small rewards are as effective as large rewards when it comes to developing new behaviors. They are more effective because you can enjoy them immediately. Gratification without delay is a key aspect of positive reinforcement. Second, make sure your reward does not work against you. Suppose you try to run every day, partly to lose weight. It makes no sense to reward yourself with a doughnut after each race. A doughnut would weaken your goal. Third, experiment. Not all rewards will motivate you in the same way. Some will be more convincing than others. For example, you may find that calling a friend is more motivating than eating a chocolate bar. If so, set your phone as a reward for completing your chosen habit. Similarly, a short walk can be more pleasant than a nap. If so, go immediately after completing the new procedure. Only by experimenting with several rewards will you find the one that suits you best. Over time, you will see designs that will inspire you in rewards. For example, you may notice that it is motivated by fun (short walks, swimming, etc.), not by food. You may notice that spending time with friends (over the phone, meeting with coffee, etc.) is more encouraging than solo lessons. As you develop new habits throughout your life, choosing rewards that inspire, you will become second nature. Don't underestimate the power of good encouragement. It can play a key role in creating new behavior patterns. In step 8, I will share a simple trick that will help you maintain the new habits you follow.

Step 8: Every day check the habit

Think about what you do at the same time every day. Here are some examples:

Brushing teeth
Take a bath
Lunch
Go to the gym
Watch your favorite TV show
Take a break from smoking
Make coffee
Go running

These actions are rooted in your mind. You do them without thinking. They are part of your daily process. As such, the omission can put you in a state of fear. This is an important feature of these daily habits. You do it every day at the same time. This, in turn, causes them to evolve in automatic responses to permanent triggers. For example, suppose you take a break to smoke every day at 10:00. You have been doing it for years. Therefore, when the clock strikes 10:00, it automatically rises and goes out with the cigarette behind the ear. This is automatic. Time, in this case, 10:00 is the trigger. Or suppose that the first thing you do after getting up in the morning is to trip over the coffee machine and turn it on. Waking up is a trigger here and get out of bed. The response to the coffee maker is automatic. This is a deep-rooted habit. Use this tactic for each new behavior you want to develop. For example, if you plan to do ten push-ups a day, do so at 7 am before going to the office. If you plan to read nonfiction for 15 minutes every day, do it during lunch. If your goal is to clean your desk every day, do it at the end of the business day. In other words, perform a new procedure at the same time every day. Does it like a clock? Put it on your daily calendar and take the time to share, even if it only takes a few minutes. From time to time, you will feel like adapting to your circumstances or emotional state (for example: "I don't want to do push-ups now. I will do it later"). Resist temptation. Executing the procedure at the same time every day makes it an automatic response to the associated trigger. In the end, you will do it without thinking. Then the routine becomes an ingrained habit that is maintained. Next: we will discuss some of the obstacles you will encounter when developing and maintaining new habits.

Step 9: Identify the traps that can sabotage

The main theme of the Little Habits revolution is to start with habits so small that it is hard not to say. Instead of doing 25 push-ups at the beginning, start with five (or only one). Instead of running a mile, start in 50 yards. You have an idea, unfortunately, no matter how small your habit, internal and external forces conspire against you. Your mind will try to convince you to neglect a new routine for more fun activities, such as taking a nap or watching television.

Unforeseen circumstances can hamper the habit. For example, a broken rope can challenge your intention to run. A low battery level of the laptop can prevent you from writing journal entries. When creating a new habit, it is important to recognize the obstacles that stand between you and success. Anticipate Get ready for them. For example, suppose you want to get used to it every day. Sometimes your mind tries to convince you that one day jumping will make you feel better.

Try to convince him to watch TV, ice cream or log in to Facebook. If you first realize that this will happen, you will be better prepared to resist temptations. Also, remember that circumstances beyond your control can also lead to a conspiracy against you. For example, I gave him a broken shoe rope. Your career plan can also depend on rain, power failures or an urgent phone conversation with your boss. If you first realize that such things can happen, you will less often give up the habit of frustration. Starting slowly and building slowly is a proven strategy to develop new behavior patterns. But he will continue to face obstacles that could jeopardize his efforts. Identify them beforehand. You will be ready to face them in a productive way that will not harm your long-term success. In the last step, we will talk about one of the most important aspects of any habits development plan: monitor progress.

Step 10: Monitoring progress once a week

This is a simple step, but it is often omitted or rejected altogether. Many people try to adopt new habits without following their progress. This is understandable; monitoring progress requires time and effort. Because so many things happen in our lives, there are few incentives. But monitoring your progress is the only way to measure how well you are doing. Remember my example of how to try to do 50 push-ups a day. I started with five a day, increasing the number by one every week. I'm 25 now. The progress I have made, or at least progress for me, is largely due to my tracking system. He accused me of responsibility. My system is not complicated. It is surprisingly simple. I keep a spreadsheet with two columns. The first column is the date. The second column is the number of bombs completed on the correct date. At first glance, I can see how far I have come and how far I have to go to reach my final goal (50 push-ups per day). Monitoring your progress does four things for you. First, it provides motivation. The more you move, the more you will be inspired by continuing with your new routine. Second, show the regularity of your habit. Remember, this should be done daily, which reinforces this as a role model. Third, monitoring progress shows what you can achieve. When I started doing push-ups, the idea of doing 25 push-ups in a row was absurd. Today is easy. I know that with constant progress, weekly falls, I will finally be able to do 50 push-ups without sweating. Fourth, when it comes to adopting new habits, good intentions are not enough. Action required the monitoring system will push you to daily activities. Many applications will help you track your progress as you develop new procedures. I prefer spreadsheets. First, they are simple and do their job perfectly. Secondly, I don't have to saturate the phone with many applications. Third, they are free (I use Google Sheets).

If you need to use the application to track your habits, here are some that I have seen that others recommend:

42Goals.com
Chains.cc
HabitGrams.com
LifeTick.com
21Habit.com
StridesApp.com
HabitList.com
Coach.me

Full disclosure: I have never used any of the above applications. I mention them only because other people like them and can have equally positive experiences. The most important thing is to monitor your progress every time you develop a new habit. It doesn't matter if you are using spreadsheets, applications or a pen and a notebook. When monitoring things. You now have a simple and proven 10-

step system that allows you to adopt a new habit that you can imagine. It works, but as the proverb says, the proof is pudding. I am ready to bet that if you use the system described, you will notice its effectiveness from the beginning. It is normal for you to experience internal resistance every time you fight for a new habit. In our brains, they like routine, and they don't like change. In Part V, we discuss the tactics that can be used to simplify the process.

MARCO STEP BY STEP

Preface suppose the lists and sequences of instructions do not apply to everyone. What a person has to do is simply experience a neighbor. This is not a bread recipe. With this in mind, take the following sequence step by step as a framework that should adapt to your situation. The specific days suggested are only a guide. More important is the progress you make when moving from one stage to the next. As we have seen, all habits, large or small, consistent or trivial, have their origin in need to automate the mind and reduce the energy needed to act. Also, when you have to get rid of an old habit, it is better to get rid of it through your next habit: movement strategy. This can be done in incremental increments as follows:

Day one to five

Spend at least one hour a day during this period wondering why you have concluded that this particular habit should be eliminated. Understand what will happen when you follow this habit. Destroy relationships? Does it affect your health? Does this affect your room? Pay attention to the effects that appear after starting this habit. At the end of these five days, you will have an exhaustive list of reasons that should motivate you to give up this habit, regardless of the discomfort it may cause at the beginning. Set the priority of this list.

Day six to ten

The next list you should do is find the factors that trigger your habit. Remember what a trigger is. This was explained earlier in the book. Take your time and make a complete list of the factors that trigger the habit. Once you understand the triggers and the reasons why you should get rid of this habit, you have two books that will help you understand each other better.

From the eleventh to the twentieth day

Between the two letters he has generated in the last ten days, he now has a basic roadmap on mental habits. Find the five triggers listed above that appear to be the most common. For example, if you smoke immediately after a meal, and this happens every time, a meal is a common trigger. Find related triggers, such as the kitchen where you eat, the food you always have or the coffee you always go to. With this in hand, start changing the habits of your associative triggers. For example, do not go to a cafeteria where you normally eat, go to a non-smoking restaurant. Change the food you eat: if you regularly eat pasta, pizza and rice, change it. Making sandwiches, the point is that it changes all the associative characteristics of the trigger. You can also perform an action. As soon as you find food in a new location, do something you usually don't do. Maybe a ride. Remember that you are not attacking your main habit, the one you are trying to quit. Now it only supports associative triggers.

Day twenty one to thirty

It is time to acquire a real habit that worries you. Remember why you have to get rid of him. After all, associative triggers are changed; the main trigger will find that it has less power to force any action. The reduced force of these circumstances would be within their willpower. The last part comes when you take all the associative triggers and the triggers and put them into a new habit. If you want to quit smoking, take something you like and look for all these triggers. Eat it at home at the table after a meal. Take it after lunch in the canteen. This is the last element of the strategy of changing habits. You can apply this to all your habits, both physical limitations and mental trajectories.

HOW TO CREATE NEW HABITS
IN JUST 30 DAYS

If you don't have the bad habit of moving around and just want to develop a new good habit, you don't have the option of using a travel strategy. Developing a new habit is as simple as having the willpower to do something consistently until habits develop. There is a better way: the image reappears, except for the stage, which we call vision. There is also willpower, except this scenario, which we call discipline. By combining vision and discipline, you have the ingredients for success. But we are not looking for exactly that yet. Our goal is action, which we want to direct the force of habit, after which it becomes easy. Imagine crawling at 4:00 in the morning. To start work, instead of suddenly opening your eyes a minute before 4:00 in the morning, M. is conscious enough and roars to leave. One is discipline; the other is a habit. As you saw in the previous chapter, habits are easy and persistent, but discipline (willpower) can disappear or get tired. Discipline consumes a lot of energy, emphasizes the psyche and can break. The habit is almost effortless, does not consume much mental energy, and there is no stress. For this reason, creating a to-do list is not as good as the habit of doing it. This question is a way of developing habits and doing it within 30 days or less. As we saw in the previous chapter, you must overcome habits in small steps. Don't make big jumps; you'll be disappointed and ruin your efforts. Creating good habits requires a proper thinking process, as in the previous chapter. In this chapter, you need reflection; in this chapter, you need visualization.

Show

Visualization is the equivalent of reflection in the creation of habits. During the reflection, observe what happened and diagnose cause and effect. In the visualization, the cause and effect are not observed, look at what you want to achieve and the step you want to take in this direction. It is different because reflection wants the past to understand when it is time to enforce what it wants. Divide your path into milestones and visualize each milestone until you reach it. When you have to make a mental effort to do something, it happens because some of you doubt how they do it. There is a way to overcome this. Visualizing yourself while doing something is an important part of doing it effortlessly and getting benefits that will reward you for doing it. As soon as you receive the reward, you can start the habit.

Small bites, check the next step and then continue. Get used to reading a book a day. (Theodore Roosevelt read three books a day, was an extraordinary player in speed). Start by dividing it by reading a chapter a day. This is your milestone. If you generally read only two or three pages a day, read the entire chapter. To see, close your eyes and see how you do what you want to achieve. Logically think about the benefits and then visualize the act. You can read the chapter. After two or three days of the chapter, go to two chapters, then three, then a slightly larger jump to five chapters, then eight chapters per day. Whenever you do, look at the previous night and then do it. Until you reach your goal of reading a book a day, when you do this, reward yourself, you must make sure you have a habit if the prize is ice cream, a movie or a meal at your favorite restaurant. Whatever it is, record yourself and then do it again. Admire until you reach the place where you would like to read a book a day. When you love him, watch how you change your mind and experience the positive aspects of your life, the act becomes easy and becomes a habit. The art of doing something consistently is a habit. If you still have to force yourself or apply discipline and effort, you can do it constantly, but this is not a habit.

Exercise and repeat

When you create a new habit, you must practice and repeat. These are not the same things. One is often confused with the other. Exercise is not just repetition. It can include repetition but also includes visualization and reflection. Repetition is only one part and consists of the constant repetition of it. To illustrate this, to become a concert pianist, practice is important. In practice, the pianist plays many times, thinks of mistakes, sets goals and then repeats everything. It will take years, but it will come. This is not a habit but a habit that lies in practice and repetition. A characteristic of the average brain is that it is influenced by repetitive things. It is like an electric motor. If you connect the battery to the cables and the current flows through the coils, it will cause movement.

On the other hand, if you remove the battery and place the voltmeter and then move the blades with your hands, you will see that the rotation produces a potential currently in the circuit. The point is that it can go both ways. The same in the brain. When something repeats, the body begins to form a mental pattern that moves towards the centre of the brain. Do you remember how the middle brain is closely related to the brainstem? When the body performs repetitive movements, it is recorded in the brainstem and returns information to the central brain. The central brain now controls how it is done. Then the next step is taken, when the reflex covers and is visualized, and the brain decides that it can be done a little differently. Have you ever hit a tennis ball and all you had to do was think about where you want to go? He didn't have to turn his arm 5 degrees or turn the torque.

You just asked for a goal, and your hand gave it to you. This is the result of the practice of repetition to create a habit. The method of repetition and exercise is a bit more primitive, but it does the job. In this case, you can't start looking, or you can't think until you see the steps, the only way that will never fail is the traditional way. Keep doing this until you join. It requires a lot of effort, but it is a sure way to turn something into a habit. This works well for those who are naturally disciplined and can put their nose on the tooth and re-peat the movement until it is blocked.

HOW TO MAKE CHANGES

Last and it all comes down to two parallel paths. The first is the ability to form good habits. The second is the ability to eliminate bad habits that creep without conscious control. Habits are an important aspect of life. They can do things effortlessly, or they can ruin their lives. They can also be fooled under the radar, causing damage without knowledge. The goal of anyone considering increasing their lives to reach a higher season or improving their mental health and happiness should be to look in the mirror and observe the actions taken and the reasons why they perform them. The easiest way to avoid bad habits is to have good habits. You only have twenty-four hours for one day and seven days a week. If you create a habit profile that represents every minute of your time, there is less chance that there is room to accumulate bad or bad habits. There are eight strategies with which we can maintain the desired habits and avoid harmful habits.

Strategy # 1

Learn to ask yourself why certain things happen to you and why you have certain habits.

Asking and taking responsibility is a practice of responsibility towards yourself. However, this is not an opportunity to cause guilt or judgment. If you can reduce your ability to judge yourself and judge others, it will give you an idea of your ability to observe yourself and your actions.

Strategy No. 2
Maintain minor changes.

The road to success is exactly this: road. It is not a jump or a jump. You must perform actions that you can perform. It always starts with something small. If you can increase the pace, do it. When you feel too tired, reduce speed. The idea is to catch up with thinking and lifestyle.

Strategy no 3
Clearly define your goals and the path you follow or not.

If your goals are clear, your subconscious will come into play and push you in that direction. If you want to get up at 4:00 every day in the future, but currently get up at 7:00, you must take small steps. Start at 6:30, go at 5:30 and so on until you reach your goal.

Strategy 4

Create a route instead of forcing the action.

It is always easier to let the surrounding forces of nature help you whenever possible. Create an environment in which these forces can be used in your favor. For example, when you have a habit of eating, change the order in the kitchen, when you eat a diet, so that a new aspect of cooking no longer activates the desire to eat.

Strategy # 5

You can create or support habits in isolation, but it becomes easier when you do it with a support group.

Therefore, the dependencies are managed in groups. Addictions have the same basic mechanisms as habits. When you create a new habit, you get a support group that regularly does what you want to adopt as a habit. If you want to read a book a day, join a club whose members are very influential readers.

Strategy No. 6

Celebrate your successes.

No matter how small your success, celebrate proportionally. When you reach a small victory, celebrate the small one. When you reach a great victory, celebrate the big one. Yes, the ceremony is an external award. This external reward is gradually spreading in his psyche.

Activate the part of the brain you see: ego. When you celebrate, you tell your subconscious that this is what you wanted.

Strategy No. 7

Movement procedures are as important as triggers and movement actions.

You can apply preexisting procedures used in other areas of your life to eliminate bad habits or bad habits that you want to eliminate.

Strategy No. 8

Don't give up; keep going.

Taking responsibility, admitting a mistake or lack of judgment and changing your behavior does not mean admitting that you are a bad person. We are all human beings, and we learn better. We learn mistakes, and a bad habit should not be the basis of a trial against you. In addition to the ways and means of creating new habits and eliminating bad habits, these eight strategies will provide additional help on your way.

HOW TO ENSURE NEW HABITS LAST

Let's make a summary. You now have a simple 10-step system that allows you to adopt new habits that you want to be part of your life. He also knows some tips and tricks that will facilitate the habit. In Part VI, we will discuss many ways to ensure that new behaviors are preserved. I mentioned some of them in previous sections. I will discuss it here in more detail and present some new ideas that will help transform desirable routines into lifelong habits.

WHY NEW HABITS ARE NOT
OFTEN OBSERVED?

Before discussing strategies that will help you maintain new habits, it is important to understand why most people have problems in this area. There are seven reasons. First, the desired procedure or behavior means too many changes. As I noted earlier, important changes cause internal resistance. The main theme of Little Habits Revolution begins with a routine so small that there is almost no internal resistance. Second, many people hit each other when they do not maintain their new habits. Their self-flagellation discourages them from further promotion. The third reason why new habits do not last is that the individual is focused on the result, not on the routine itself. Our brain responds to a consistent application. Therefore, the procedures performed daily at the same time, guided by the same triggers, become deeply rooted habits. On the contrary, when our approach changes from routine to result, we lose momentum, and our responses to specific triggers become less automatic. Fourth, we lose sight of our reasons for adopting new procedures. Without clear reasons to continue, we lose sight of our goal and eventually abandon our new positive behaviors. Fifth, many people do not follow good habits because they neglect to create a favorable environment. For example, a person who wants to start jogging in the morning wakes up late. A person who wants to follow a healthy diet keeps cookies, chips and ice cream at home. The environment plays an important role in determining whether a habit persists. The sixth reason why habits are not maintained is that people often try to adopt too many at once. We will discuss the importance of maintaining the practice Part V: Seven principles to prepare for success (principle No. 3). Running for several at a time is a recipe for failure. Seventh, many people do not take their habits seriously. They start with good intentions but are not completely attached to them. Not carrying out new procedures during the next few days is not a serious matter for them. Therefore, they do not want to find the reasons for their negligence or are not motivated to find a solution. Leaving new procedures is inevitable when they encounter internal resistance. Now he knows the problems to consider if he has difficulties in maintaining new habits. If you have difficulties, review the seven reasons above. Check if any of them describe your circumstances. If so, take the necessary steps to solve them.

Use for responsibility

It is worth coming back here in the context of choosing a good and responsible partner. A good partner will encourage you to develop new behaviors and encourage you to change them to lifestyle habits. There are five key factors to consider when choosing this person.

First, you must be prepared to give good and honest intentions. Remember that you will probably stumble sometimes. It will not help you to be responsible for someone who does not want to make constructive and supportive comments that will help you return to normal. Second, find someone who can honestly support your efforts. For example, if you want to get used to reading nonfiction books, choose someone who likes to do the same. This person will be delighted with the new habit and more committed to success. Third, choose a partner that wants to connect several times a week, preferably every day. It allows you to report your habit every day, especially if you did that day or not. It is useful to plan the connection time. For example, text us every day at noon if you plan to get used to it in the morning. Connect at the end of the business day if you plan to do so during lunch. Fourth, choose a responsible partner that challenges you. For example, suppose you want to do 25 push-ups a day (starting with just five push-ups a day). When he turns 25, a good partner will ask if he plans to go to 30. And then to 35. And so on. Fifth, if possible, choose a partner who is trying to adopt the same habit as you. For example, if you want to start jogging, be responsible for someone who wants to do the same. In turn, this person can be held responsible. Imagine how encouraging it will be to work with a trusted partner to develop the same habit at the same pace. They can keep up with the daily SMS messages:

You: "I chased 500 yards in the morning. And " Partner: "Me too! 600 yards still are made tomorrow? "She: "Of course! :)" partner

"Very They have a good night!" LA responsibility it can be fun and challenging. The key is to choose a partner that is consistent, supportive and encouraging when you try to transform your new behaviors into deeply rooted habits.

Connect your new habit with a reliable signal

We talked about the importance of triggers or signals in Part II: triggers, procedures, rewards and loops. You learned about the different types of triggers (time, position, mental state, people and previous events), as well as the role they play in encouraging us to act. In step 4 of Part IV: 10 steps to model long-term healthy habits! We care about the selection of factors that complement our objectives. To use the example in this section, you can put running shoes near the bed if you want to run in the morning. The correct trigger would be to see your shoes awake. Or you can floss immediately after brushing your teeth. Brushing your teeth would complement the use of dental floss. In both cases, the signal sets the scene for the new procedure. Choosing triggers as an aspect of habit development is so important that it is worth visiting again. Choosing the right triggers can make the difference between practicing the habit as an automatic response and the daily fight against internal resistance. The perfect trigger is what you control. For example, you must dictate the position of the shoes. Decide whether to brush your teeth or not. These circumstances are not affected by external factors. You check them. Thanks to this, they are reliable. You can count on them. If you get used to the day, you are independent of other people and events. Some signals will affect you more than others. It is important to test different signals to determine which ones are right for you. For example, suppose you want to get used to doing push-ups every day. You may experience the following triggers: Wash your face. Drink a glass of water. Listen to your favorite Bon Jovi song.

Turn on the television to watch the morning news.

After trying several triggers, you will discover that one of them triggers the other, encouraging them to act. You should use it. The most important aspect is to check if there is a trigger. For example, if you live in an area where there is a significant amount of rainfall, avoid using the word "return home after a short walk" as a signal to perform daily push-ups. You can't control the weather. As a result, there will be times when you will not be able to walk, which makes it an incredible trigger. Don't underestimate the importance of choosing memory when introducing new procedures in your day.

Insert the new procedure into the existing habit stack

It is the practice of anchoring new procedures in existing habits. It is an effective method to maintain new procedures. It works like this: there are many things you do during the day. You do them without thinking. Some are connected or stacked on top of each other. For example, consider the morning routine. After waking up, you can stumble in the bathroom to wash your face, brush your teeth, use the bathroom and take a shower. This series of activities have many habits. After getting out of the shower, you can dry, dress and dry your hair. This is another pile of habits. After leaving the bathroom, you can pour yourself a cup of coffee, toast a slice of bread, mix eggs and check your email. This is another group. You probably have many habits every day, even if you rarely think about it. Your brain has created connections between individual habits, which makes each of them an automatic response to the previous ones. One of the most effective ways to develop a new habit is to place it in an existing pile. Your brain will quickly create a new connection between the new routine and the habits that support it. We will illustrate this idea with our example of "push-ups push-ups".

THINK ABOUT THESE POSITIVE EFFECTS
OF THE NEW HABIT

Risking us to defeat a dead horse, we act on purpose. This is necessary to understand in the context of the development of habits. Everything we do, each of our actions are motivated by a specific intention. The same applies to the proactive adoption of new behaviors. We practice being fit. We eat healthy foods to reduce the risk of heart and vascular problems. We read nonfiction to learn about topics that are a mystery to us. Of course, he hopes he benefits from each new habit in a certain way. Maybe you are waiting for more concentration and productivity. More energy may be needed during the business day. Perhaps you would like to strengthen the relationships you share with your spouse and children. The expected benefits encourage daily activities. Get inspired to follow the procedures you think will be followed. Unfortunately, it is easy to forget how your new positive behaviors will affect your life. When this happens, it is more likely to give up. You are more likely to give up habits that will have the desired effect. In step 10 of Part IV: 10 steps to develop healthy habits that last! I recommend checking your progress once a week. It will motivate you, reveal the correctness of the new routine and show you what you can achieve. This review session is the perfect time to consider how the new procedures will improve your quality of life. For example, how does an increase in afternoon energy levels affect performance? How will a healthy diet affect your well-being during the day? How does a new vision of a topic that fascinates you read nonfiction books work? Recognizing how your life will improve after adopting a new habit will remind you why you try so hard. Whether you are healthier, happier, safer or more connected with your loved ones, the reminder can be a strong incentive to act. And this can help eliminate internal resistance by incorporating new and healthy procedures into everyday experiences.

Now he has everything he needs to develop positive habits that enrich his life. You can start at any time, even now. If you are not sure what habits to use, read on. At the beginning of part VII, I will describe 23 examples of habits.

Examples of habits can be developed using these small strategic habits

I gave you a complete and proven system to adopt every habit you choose. Millions of people have used some form of strategy in the ten steps described in this book to apply a new positive routine that they have a better quality of life. You can experience the same success. The challenge is knowing where to start. There are innumerable habits that you can develop that will enrich your life. But it can be paralyzing as an amplifier. To help you get started, I will list 23 habits that can lead to a more satisfying lifestyle. My goal is not to dictate habits to follow. On the contrary, it is the starting point for brainstorming that can have the greatest impact on your life.

LITTLE HABITS THAT CAN
CHANGE YOUR LIFE

For each of the following procedures, I will present some ideas on how to start small. After all, this is the main theme of the revolution of small habits. Remember that the key is to start from so small that it is difficult to reject it. I would like to emphasize one last time that my goal is not to suggest one of the following habits. Instead, use this section as a tool to launch your ideas. I hope that the 23 habits listed below can help you brainstorm as part of the routine changes that will cause a dramatic and positive change in your life.

1 - Breakfast Most of us grew up listening to this advice.

Although it is doubtful that breakfast is the most important meal of the day, its benefits cannot be denied. We enjoy more energy, better focus and easier weight control (to name a few). The problem is that the hustle and bustle of our lives often discourage us from reserving 15 minutes for breakfast. Our mornings are in a hurry, and the first meal of the day is usually a victim of our busy schedules. Get used to eating something nutritious in the morning, even if that means getting up 15 minutes earlier. How to start from an early age: eat orange, apple or banana every day during the first week. These products require minimal preparation. Cook hard-boiled eggs in the second week. Add a slice of toast in the third week. (Note: adapt to your intolerance or personal sensitivity to food).

2 - Practice active listening

This is a great development habit if you value interpersonal and communication skills. You can strengthen the relationships you share with the people in your life. The state can also be the most effective leader in your work. Active listening focuses on what the person says. Instead of letting the mind wander or think about the right answer, we listen carefully to the other person's message. This ensures that we interpret it correctly. How to start with something small: active practice listening during short and irrelevant conversations in the first two weeks. These include conversations that you like with strangers. They probably consist of small conversations, so they will have little effect on the omission of details. During the third and fourth week, practice with people you often see, but not necessarily an important part of your life. Examples include waiters at a local coffee shop and employees of your favorite grocery store. Practice active listening with friends and loved ones since the fifth week. These conversations tend to be more intimate, with the level of confidence higher.

3 - Do push-ups, abdominal muscles and squats

You know that exercise is important. It plays an important role in maintaining good health. Unfortunately, this is one of the first activities that we put in the background when our lives change, or we feel tired. But it's easy to keep in the habit of staying fit. How to start with something small: the first practice in your daily calendar or to-do list. The program, according to a reliable activator. Then choose a form of exercise and decide a small number of repetitions. For example, you can choose push-ups and select five. To create a program that shows how the habit will develop over time. When I started doing push-ups, I increased the number of repetitions by one per week. It worked for me. Do the same with each type of exercise you choose.

4 - Master the art of conversation

Establishing a conversation is an art that takes time and effort to master. It's not about saying what you might think. It is rather the art of gently developing a conversation towards the pleasure and commitment of all parties. It requires active listening, recognizing mutual interests and recognizing the body and another language.

It also means avoiding habitual conversation killers, such as interrupting people and monopolizing the spotlight. Through practice, you can become a colloquial ninja. First steps with your daughter: during the first two weeks focus on reducing the number of mistakes made during conversations. For example, if you tend to discuss, try to stop this trend. If you speak too fast, work to reduce speed. In the third week, practice the aspect of a good conversation. An example would be to ask useful questions related to the experience of a conversation partner. Alternatively, focus on maintaining a fair distribution of how much each party contributes to the conversation. Practice an additional aspect every week to gradually develop your skillset.

5 - Drink more water

Most of us don't drink enough water. It's not that we don't like it. We do not think about it or prefer other drinks (soft drinks, coffee, etc.). But increasing water consumption has many advantages. Improves digestion, kidney function and mood. It helps our immune system and helps stop fatigue. Drinking more water can also help us control our weight. If you don't drink enough, think about how you can increase your daily intake. How to start with something small: drink a small glass of water immediately after getting up in the morning. If you take afternoon naps, do the same. Always carry a bottle of water with you. Those available in bulk in supermarkets generally contain 17.5 oz. Try to drink half a bottle every day during week 1. Drink a full bottle every day during week 2. Continue adding half a bottle, approximately 9 ounces, over the next few weeks. Buy a larger bottle of water: at Amazon, many good options grow for less than $ 20 as consumption increases. I bought from you, my bottle of 24 oz for $ 12.

6 - Write in a personal diary

Many people swear to write a diary. They claim that it helps them generate ideas, develop complex concepts and increase their self-discipline. Some say it is a game key role to help them achieve their goals. Countless historical figures with an impressive reputation kept personal diaries. These include Albert Einstein, Mark Twain, Thomas Edison, Herman Melville, Thomas Jefferson, Leonardo da Vinci, George S. Patton and Charles Darwin. It is tempting to keep a personal diary if only to follow in their footsteps. The question is: how to start if writing is not easy for you? Of course, when you start small! How to start with something small: write 50 words every day during the first week. Increase production to 100 words per day during week 2. Continue increasing the number of words you write by 50 per day at the beginning of each new week. In within a few months to keep the habit of writing every day, and he voices with little internal resistance.

7 - Praise from strangers.

Everyone likes to receive compliments. But few people have the same pleasure in giving them to others. A good habit is a development, if only for selfish reasons. Complementary strangers will make you look more attractive, help you build trust and improve your perspective on life. And the best part? It doesn't cost a penny. Adopting this behavior can be difficult for introverts and scammers. Take it slowly and increase over time. How to start at an early age: spend two weeks congratulating strangers a day. Be honest. Don't pretend you love shoes if you think they are ugly. Make two compliments a day at weeks 3 and 4. Starting with the fifth week, increase the daily number to three and join friends and family. Do it personally. It is not important to make compliments by SMS, phone or email.

8 - Take short walks.

Everyone likes to walk. If so, it allows us to get out of our backs and enjoy the fresh air. It is also a great form of low impact exercise; Even if you don't sweat, you still move your body.

The challenge is to take the time to walk. Even the short ones. Many of us are so involved in the daily activities that we stop dealing with activities that we consider most urgent. However, consider: daily short walks will improve metabolism, reduce stress and help you control your weight. It can even stop osteoporosis. Given these advantages, it may be time to adopt this habit. Here we will show you how to: Start: take two 5-minute walks each day of the first week. Extend the duration of each gear to 10 minutes from the second week. Keep the same duration in week 3, but increase the number of daily walks to three. From week 4, the duration of each walk increases to 15 minutes. Begin four walks a day in week 5. Until then, you will walk for one hour a day. It is more exercise than most people!

9 - Read nonfiction books

Reading nonfiction is a completely different experience than reading fiction. None of them is better than the other. These different essays only expose us to new ideas and concepts. In the form of autobiography and memories, it gives us an idea of the lives of those who preceded us. In the form of essays, it exposes us to the observation and reasoning of others. In the form of scientific journals, it presents several unknown disciplines, from biology to zoology. Reading nonfiction is not just about collecting data. He delves into a topic that fascinates us with the hope of learning new things. If you are not used to reading nonfiction books, getting started can be difficult. This is a difficult development habit. For this reason, it is important to start small. How to start with something small: read five minutes a day during the first week. Increase time to 10 minutes a day in the second week. Beginning in the third week, read 10 minutes a day in the morning and 10 minutes a day at night. In week 4, increase the duration of each reading session to 15 minutes a day. In the fourth week, you will read, and I hope you enjoy it! - half an hour of daily reading.

10 - Clean your workplace.

Improve your concentration skills; it makes you less susceptible to interference; Lower your stress level and feel more relaxed. And, of course, you spend less time looking for things. So, if your desk is a disaster, you may wonder what the best way to get rid of the mess is. Some recommend that you plan your initiative worldwide for waste disposal and advise you to give it a few hours. As you can probably imagine, I recommend the opposite approach. How to start with something small: discard or store an item per day for the first two weeks. That is no longer meant. Beginning in the third week, discard or store two items a day. In week 4, increase to three per day. Beginning in the fifth week, discard or save the object each time you leave the desk. Assuming you take occasional breaks, this will ensure that several incorrect items are repaired each day. The reason I urge you to do this is that it creates a procedure. Instead of eliminating all the chaos in a 3- hour window, develop a cleaning habit. Therefore, it is more likely to keep the desk clean in the long term.

11 - the smile of people, for some smile is natural.

We smile at everyone we meet, friends or strangers. Others among us are more hesitant. They smile only when justified. What if smiling is good for your health? Wouldn't you try to do it more often? Scientific studies show that a smile can reduce stress, which in turn helps the heart. This causal effect was demonstrated in a study published in the journal Psychological Science in 2012. Suppose we want to develop a habit. Here we show you how to do it. How to start from an early age: smile at (extra) people every day during the first week. Focus on strangers and friends. For example, smile at the people you know while waiting in the Starbucks line. Smile at the supermarket checkout. Increase the number of people you smile with each week. At the end of the third month, you will gain a reputation as one of the friendliest people in your city.

12 – Meditation

Meditation is known to reduce stress, pain and anxiety. People who practice this regularly also say they can sleep better, are more aware and relaxed. Some even say that meditation helped them overcome depression. In short, there are many reasons to try. The question is: how to start? Start small: the biggest obstacle that most people face in meditation is sitting for a long time. They become restless. Start sitting still for 60 seconds. At this point, focus on breathing and presence. Do it every day in the first week. Extend the session time to two minutes at week two and three minutes at week 3. Extend the session one minute a week. Set 10 minutes as a goal. There is plenty of time to enjoy the health benefits of meditation.

13 - Wake up before you hurt me.

Getting up early in the morning allows me to do more things. I can work alone without worrying about a phone call, unexpected visits from friends and family, or countless distractions that could disturb my impulse. Maintaining a high level of performance is important to me. I bet this is also important for you. Getting up early is one of the easiest ways. I encourage you to try. How to start with something small: set the alarm five minutes earlier than normal. Do it every morning in the first week. In the second week, reset the alarm for another five minutes. Come back another five minutes in the third week. At this point, you get up 15 minutes before. This is not a bad start. Continue setting the alarm five minutes every week. You will wake up an hour earlier in three months. Because it works at small intervals of 5 minutes, you won't feel hit by an 18-wheeler.

14 - Express your gratitude

You have probably heard the phrase "adopt an attitude of gratitude." I laughed when I heard that because it seemed vague. But since then I have learned that thanks to regular thanks you can earn a lot. It affects my mood and my vision of life. It relaxes me, makes me more optimistic and controls my stress level. Expressing gratitude makes me feel better, which probably has a positive effect on my health. It didn't come naturally to me. I had to get used to that. If you want to do the same, I recommend this approach. How to start with something small: write three things for which you are grateful. Do it at the beginning of each day for a week. In the second week, write three articles a day, but I also thank the person. You can do it in person, by email or by text message. You decide. The key is that you do it every day. From week 3, increase the number of written items to five. Continue to express your gratitude to one person per day. Select the day of the week, for example, Sunday to see your written notes. You will have a list of 35 positive elements for reflection. Imagine how this can affect your mood!

15 - Keep in touch with friends.

Our friends improve our lives. They form a support network in which we can count on difficult times. They also serve as a support team when we succeed. Spending time with friends makes us feel more connected, which gives us a sense of satisfaction. The problem is that we live intensely. Among our responsibilities at home and in the workplace, it is often difficult to keep contacts alive. We tell each other that we should call our friends and organize dinner, but the call will never be made, and the date will never be set. This is the challenge that most of us face. The good news is that it is easy to keep in touch with friends after developing a habit. How to do it. Follow these steps: Start: send an email to your friend weekly. Select a day and insert tasks in your calendar. Let it be a repetitive element. Do this for eight weeks, meeting several friends every week. From week 9, send two emails per week. At this point, you will connect with eight friends a month. We hope to have the opportunity to see this.

They personally on the road. I recommend sending an email instead of a text message. It is more personal, communicates more interest and allows your thoughts to be expressed better. # 16 - Help people who show kindness to others for the benefit of you and them. Think about it the last time you helped someone who was in trouble. There it didn't help you feel good? Science says it is a natural side effect of producing someone's day. We feel good when we do good. If you are not used to helping people, try to develop a habit. You will be surprised how beautiful it is for you and the world around you. I will treat it this way. How to start with something small: write a list of many ways you can help someone. Your list may include charitable donations, caring for a friend's son, walking a neighbor's dog or teaching someone new skills. There are countless ways to show kindness to both friends and strangers. With this list, you will never lose how you help others. Try to help someone every day. Offering help does not require much time or effort. For example, pick up newspapers from neighbors if many have gathered at the entrance. An offer to pay for a person's drink at Starbucks. You don't have to increase the number of people you help every day. If I did, I could spend the whole day helping others at the expense of their performance. If you decide to follow this habit, your development is more important than the number of people you help.

17 - Track how you spend your time

Have you ever felt time pass between your fingers? You start every day with the hope that you will do a lot to end up frustrated. Worse, if you do not track time, it is likely to be clear how this happened. What is done is difficult or even impossible to make improvements.

I strongly believe in tracking how I use my time every day. From direct experience, I know I waste a lot if I don't follow it. My productivity is falling. If you have never used your time, try it. You may discover that you are wasting time that could otherwise be used to develop projects, grow your business or spend time with your family. Getting used to it is not difficult. But it requires consistent action. Many people stumble there. Here is the approach that I recommend.

How to start with something small: create an account on Toggl.com (it's free). Track your use of time during the day. If it takes five minutes to review on Facebook, save it. If you go for a walk for 15 minutes, continue. If you work tirelessly for two hours, write it down. Verify how time has passed. Think about where you can customize things. For example, you can spend 12 sessions of 5 minutes on Facebook, Twitter and Instagram. It's an hour; you can decide to reduce this time in half. After reviewing the first day and making corrections, go to the second day. Then look for areas that still need modification. Do this until you feel comfortable with the way you spend your time. When you feel comfortable, do weekly checks to make sure the time you spend with you is correct.

18 - Learn new things

Learning new things makes us more interesting for others. We become better interlocutors when we can intelligently discuss a wider range of topics. It also keeps boredom at a distance. The brain develops thanks to new ideas, concepts and facts. Try to establish a connection between what you know and the new things you learn. You will also discover that learning new things puts you in touch with people with whom you would not otherwise interact. I enjoyed many conversations with strangers on various topics. Some of these strangers became friends. How to develop the habit of learning new things? As you can imagine, I recommend you start with something small. Start with something small: create a list of websites that publish articles on many different topics. Examples include MentalFloss.com, TheAtlantic.com, Mashable.com and Priceonomics.com. Visit one page a day and read a short article. Do it every day for a month. Keep a list of new things you learn. Look at the end of the month. You will be surprised by the variety of materials you read about. Imagine what you will learn in a year by simply reading a short article a day!

19 - Save You already know many reasons to save.

This helps to finance your retirement. It also ensures that financial resources are available to cope with life curves (for example, the urgent need for a new national ceiling). Saving money also helps to reserve funds for short-term use. For example, you can take a family vacation, start a business or buy a 98-inch 4K Ultra HD 3D 4K LED TV from which you can drool. It is difficult for many people to save money. Not because they are struggling to make ends meet. Rather, reserving money every month is a difficult habit.

Development during shopping offers the promise of immediate satisfaction. So how do you get used to saving? Of course, when you start small! How to start with something small: open a savings account and reserve $ 10 for each withdrawal. If you get paid every two weeks, do it for two months. If you receive a monthly scholarship, do so for four months. At the end of this initial period, increase the amount reserved for each withdrawal to $ 20. Do so for two months (or four months if you receive a monthly scholarship). Then increase the amount of USD 30. You may think: "At this rate, save me five years to save enough money to take my family on vacation!" But the point is to develop the habit of saving. After the habit has taken root, you can increase the amount you save each month to a number that supports your goals. At this point, the habit will be deeply rooted, which will help maintain consistency.

20 - Use the time fragmentation method is a time management strategy and increased productivity.

It involves organizing the day in several short periods and assigning these fragments to specific tasks. For example, you can spend 30 minutes writing blog posts, 20 minutes reading and receiving emails and 45 minutes answering phone calls. Each action would have its time. It is better to plan brief gaps between the individual elements so that the brain can rest. This strategy makes it less susceptible to interference and more susceptible to working in a variable state. I use it personally, and I noticed that my performance had increased significantly. The challenge is that the time fragmentation method becomes part of your day. For most people, this is not natural. But you can learn it and become a habit of continuous exercise. If you want to use this method to reduce time during the day, use this approach. How to start at an early age: Create a list of activities you plan to work on this week. Check your daily or weekly calendar if you have one. Or check your to-do lists. During the first week, assign two short fragments (for example, 30 minutes or less) to two specific activities each day. From week 2, add the fragment for the third time and assign the appropriate activity. Add a quarter to week three and fifth week to week 4. Add more time fragments, one an extra week until the end of the day. This progress will allow you to get used to sharing the day and work without distractions. In two months, the habit will take root, and you will see an unusual impact on performance.

21 - Start each day with the list of things to do.

I strongly believe in the use of homework lists as a guide to how I spend my time every day. Many people use to-do lists in some way, even if this involves using a long to-do list. (I recommend a complete list of tasks system that encourages the use of several lists. This system takes into account the context and other factors). A common mistake is to create such lists in response to a busy day. For example, a person can come to the office and realize that he has many tasks to solve. This person immediately creates a list of activities that describes each activity in detail. There is a much better approach: make a to-do list the night before. When you wake up the next morning, you'll know exactly what you need to achieve. There will be no feeling of sudden despair. This is how you would develop this habit. How to start with something small: create a list of daily activities with up to three elements. Do this every night before bedtime for a week. The next day, focus on doing three things on your daily list. From the second week, increase the number of items in the daily list to four. Play your bedtime lists every night. Then, commit to removing each action from the list the next day. During the third week, increase the number of items in the task list to five. As before, create lists the night before and dedicate to each activity the next day. Continue creating lists with five exercises a day for the next five weeks. After eight weeks of daily use, you will develop the habit of using to-do lists, as well as the habit of creating them before bedtime. The routine will become second nature.

22 - Learn to breathe properly

Although breathing is easy, proper breathing requires considerable effort. It involves deep breathing; this practise is sometimes called diaphragmatic breathing, not short, shallow sips of air that most of us get used to.

CONCLUSION

Habits are in all of us and exist at all levels of human psychology. Everything in us is based on a pre-existing algorithm made by something internal, external or both. Famine at noon is also a habit. The need for morning coffee is a habit. The group of people who had regular eating habits in the morning was divided into two groups. One group received coffee in which caffeine was deactivated, the other did not receive coffee, but tea with additional caffeine, whose concentration was similar to daily consumption. The only consistent thing is that they get their hot drinks every morning. The group, which did not have caffeine, but planned to drink only coffee, spent all day without withdrawal symptoms, except for a slightly reduced level of activity. The second group that thought they were not drinking caffeine but were drinking caffeine in tea was mainly lethargic and unproductive. The study showed that, although a chemical element is formed in the caffeine reaction, a large proportion of the reaction was common. If someone drinks coffee for so long, the body (from a chemical point of view) has already become resistant to the dose; the actual abandonment is ending the habit. To overcome these factors, the transfer of coffee with tea sometimes helps to maintain a habit but changes dependence on something that has different properties and amounts of stimulants. The point is that habits play with the mind, and you have to be prepared to face it. Fasting is one of the best ways to learn how the body reacts to a habit. Eating is regular exercise. From a physiological point of view, the body does not need three meals a day. But when dinner time comes and there is no habit of eating, the body begins to show symptoms that make you think of hunger. Remember that the centre of habits has direct control over our brainstem, which controls all the physiological symptoms that alert. When you fast, you do two things. First, it allows you to concentrate on the strength of body sensations. After a while, the average brain gives up and stops causing discomfort. However, the benefit, in the context of habits, reveals your body and how it responds to the cessation of your most precious habit: food. When you develop control over your habit, understand the basic mechanisms and practice different strategies, you will find that your habit profile is different in many aspects from others. They can still help by sharing their experiences and can be a source of support but a path to victory.

CPSIA information can be obtained
at www.ICGtesting.com
Printed in the USA
BVHW041013150321
602551BV00006B/477

9 781008 993141